Karma Wisdom for Conscious Living Understanding Complex Causality for Wiser Choices

KARMA WISDOM FOR CONSCIOUS LIVING :KARMA AND THE LAW OF ATTRACTION

First edition. February 16, 2024.

Copyright © 2024 Loryan wenny.

ISBN: 979-8224181094

Written by Loryan wenny.

Table of Contents

Introduction

Since the beginning of human civilization, there has been a search to make sense of life and discover deeper truths about our existence. A question that has captivated spiritual seekers, philosophers, and ordinary people trying to understand life's ups and downs Is: What invisible forces or universal laws might influence the unfolding of events, the patterns In our lives, the good fortune we receive or harsh knocks that come our way? Over millennia, the concept of karma has emerged in Indian, Buddhist and East Asian schools of philosophy as a law of moral causation that can help provide answers.

The word karma has Its roots in ancient Sanskrit and Pali languages. It translates as "action" or "deed", but more broadly signifies the entire cycle of causation that governs existence. Simply put, karma links intentional actions to future results. It Is a natural law of cause and effect, the repercussions of thoughts, words and actions that sent out ripples into the Interconnected cosmic fabric of creation. Karma draws connections between actions in the past, present realities, and possibilities for the future. So this vast concept provides a framework for making sense of life's apparent disparities and inequalities. Why do some people face more misfortune than fortune? What leads to differences In talents, character, circumstances people are born into, even the length of their lives? An understanding of karma provides insight.

The workings of karma are precise, intricate and complex because so many dynamics are at play. Our personal actions initiate karma, but external situations also come back to us as results of distinct or indiscernible causes. Family, community, global and even cosmic karma cycles move alongside shaping events. And what happens when natural disasters hit – is there collective karma at play? How much individual free will exists alongside karmic destinies? So while the cycle seems straightforward, its practice is complicated. This book will unravel some of these dynamics. By viewing life through the lens of karma, we open to greater wisdom, .compassion and peace

Four Key Principles of Karma

Intentional action initiates karma: According to the Buddha's teachings in the Pali scriptures, karma specifically refers to intention or volition behind an action. So beyond just deeds, underlying motivations matter when karma gets generated. For example, giving money to charity out of genuine care creates positive karma, while giving only for recognition may not yield the same fruit. Subtle intentions behind thoughts and words also have .effects

.

Karma ripens as effects: Once initiated, karma will bear fruit whenever conditions are right. As observed in forest ecosystems, when seeds meet suitable conditions, they grow. So we may be planting karmic seeds continually through our actions. Specific effects follow cause, but may sometimes skip generations. There are .also collective societal karma cycles affecting groups

NATURE AND QUALITY of actions vary: Skillful, morally wholesome acts like being generous, ethical, wise and kind create good karma. While clearly harmful deeds generating anger, greed, delusion or violence lead to undesirable results. More complex mixed actions yield mixed fruits. Even good intentions can sometimes accidentally cause harm, setting up negative chains. So .understanding nuances offers more insight

Karma intensifies over cycles of rebirth: Karma gets more intricate in theories around the cycle of reincarnation or rebirth adopted by Hindu, Buddhist and other Dharmic faiths. The idea suggests an evolving soul's karmic residues carry over beyond one lifetime, leading to new births and deaths. People reborn with unfortunate life circumstances might have unskillful karma accrued previously ripening. Ideas about ending rebirth cycles .through enlightenment underlie Indian religious thought

THIS SIMPLIFIED YET solution-oriented book will dive deeper into these key principles from karma theories and explore what they teach us. How might this universal paradigm help navigate inequities or life struggles with more wisdom, self-responsibility, and compassion? Are there ways for individuals and society to rewrite unwholesome karma cycles and consciously cultivate more ethical, positive systems? What meaningful philosophies and practices around karma have stood the test of centuries? What aspects need re-examination based on new collective understandings emerging around social justice? How might contemplating nature's mysterious karmic chain of interconnectedness inspire more purposeful living? These questions and reflections hope to offer a constructive view of harmonizing personal karma with the profound goal of alleviating .suffering for all beings

The ubiquity of karma is evident when you hear people of all walks of life say things like "what goes around comes around" or "you reap what you sow". Whether used humorously when someone faces consequences or mentioned solemnly when ethical failures plague corrupt leaders; karma has become a cultural shorthand for life's inscrutable moral balancing. Behind the casual references, this ancient Eastern paradigm offers a profoundly unique lens to reflect on the seeming injustice of fate, making sense of life's vicissitudes. Beyond superficial understandings, the philosophical underpinnings provide nuanced frameworks for self-cultivation and realizing one's highest purpose within humanity's shared existence.

What makes karma remarkable is how it straddles worldly everyday realities and sublime transcendent truth. Most religions grapple with explaining stark disparities in human experience – why some people face abundant misfortune and others fortuitous blessings. Dharmic teachings go beyond offering solace that difficulties might secure better rebirth, providing urgent ethical guidance for this life. The Buddha notably urged not speculating on metaphysical matters but to awaken to present reality within impermanence. So while intricate cosmological constructs around karma persist across Indian thought, radical teachings also redirect to ethical living and alleviating palpable suffering. If intention fuels action, karma applies to every choice confronting us – do I lash out with harsh words? Do I offer compassion to struggling neighbors? Understanding this relentless chain questioning what ripens from volition makes karma intensely personal.

Prince Siddartha renounced regal comforts seeking essential truths after stark spiritual encounters with aging, sickness, death and ascetic deprivation. Why such disparity? What allows some beings joy while others endure immense pain? Does a path exist that transcends this suffering? These questions compelled his enlightened insights. Core Buddhist principles of interdependence, impermanence and non-self signify that nothing exists independently allowing inequalities to persist indefinitely. By infusing experiences with intention and effort focused on wisdom and compassion, personal karma gets aligned to universal liberation from deluded egocentric patterns causing anguish to oneself and others. Every Buddhist school revolves around skillfully manifesting this vision of existence as an ethical opportunity.

Hindu cosmologies envelop staggering timescales spanning millions of years and intricately constructed lokas (realms). The Puranas describe our current era Kali Yuga as an age of discord after Dharma, righteous order personified by the bull god progressively weakens through the rotating four cycles of existence over 311 trillion years! Within this unimaginably vast canvas, immortal souls (atman) transmigrate through stages of reincarnation (samsara) across realms like Deva godly planes or Naraka purgatorial hells. Furthermore, ideas in Ayurveda equate karma from past lives (prarabdha) to congenital health conditions, even insects infestations to homegrown produce! Jainism similarly embraces strict non-violence (ahimsa) to avoid accruing harm and binding karma matter (dravya karma) polluting the deathless jiva soul aiming for purification (moksha). The performance of intricate vows, fasting and penance among Shramanic traditions indicates deep consideration to karmic consequences of intentional actions however small. Consistent across schools is upholding Dharma through one's life stage duty (svadharma) without attachment to personal results.

So intricately embedded across generations, karma has permeated family and community traditions in India and wider Asia Buddhist cultures deep into heritage Southeast Asian kingdoms like Srivijaya or Angkor Wat temples, old Tibetan monasteries to modern cities like Bangkok, Shanghai or Tokyo. Daily activities consciously connect to unseen kinetics – from leaving temple offerings to feeding strays, burning incense to masked dances reenacting myths. Cultural practices bring visible form to karmic currents, channeling them to blessing receive rather than burdensome fate. Holi colors celebrating spring's arrival act as public purge. Solah Somvar fasts appeal to Shiva asking for desired fortunes. While violent or oppressive acts also risk backlash curse across generations. There is rich creative interplay between devotion invoking grace versus cautious concession to sublime forces personified as gods or guru's authority. These nuances around action and result often mystify outsider perspectives seeking neat linear equations yet yield valuable holistic wisdom when one embraces broader vistas including unseen influences.

While origin narratives differ on precise workings, karma broadly invokes moral equilibrium across life's unevenness. Some crystallizing passages from the Upanishadic scriptures capture its essence:

"According to one's action, according to what one does, so one becomes. The doer of good becomes good. The doer of evil becomes evil."(Brhadaranyaka Upanishad 4.4.5)

"A man turns into something according to his deeds and actions."(Chandogya Upanishad 5.10.7)

These pithy verses illustrate simply yet profoundly how qualities manifesting inwardly connect to what gets mirrored outwardly across visible lifetimes or fleeting moments. Why exactly we experience fortune or misfortune differs based on varied Hindu and Buddhist interpretations. Broadly the chain links intentional choice, action and result while precisely attributing causal factors varies – ranging from fatalistic destiny, hereditary advantage, current environment, other beings impact or interactions between previous and present karma. Fundamentally however, volitional action translates to moral habit which shapes reality. Carefully considering this empowers conscious choice.

While mechanically linking karma to visible reward or punishment lends itself to potential misconceptions, the theory's subtlety also allows reformulating injustice or structural oppression arising from willful ignorance or harmful intent. When we set out wanting happiness yet cause unskillful actions violating ethical principles (silas) like truthfulness, responsible sexuality or spiritual commitments, negative consequences will follow teaching us discernment. Equally if social barriers limit access and opportunities for particular groups despite inborn talents and effort made, collective determination properly channeled can rewrite those karmic patterns towards justice and equality for all. There is practical urgency in this for systemic change. Volition gets powerfully unleashed as movements gather force to oppose unjust laws until views progress realigning to long arc of righteousness. So properly understood, karma forms a basis for non-violent activism or spiritual radicalism seeking moral truth. This vision stirs compassionate response to suffering rather than indifference, of our fates being profoundly interdependent.

While originating in ancient Asian worldviews, contemporary thinkers also examine integrating karma philosophies with current science, psychology or social reform. Some hypotheses equating karma to laws of physics like magnetism and nested complexity theory lend themselves to falsifiable models. Cultural discussion continues on dismantling unjust privilege, healing intergenerational trauma and affirming gender fluidity across overlapping marginalized identities also framed as positive karmic disruption to dogmas once used to justify oppression. Integrating spiritual discernment with secular ethics offers promise for progress.

Ultimately the universality of consequences from volition being inescapable holds a mirror reminding to walk the path more mindfully, speak words more kindly and extend help readily to lighten another's burden. For when we uplift even humble creatures who crawl the earth or meek trees yielding fruit season after season simply by being, ripples too subtle to trace imprint somewhere meaningful. This mindset shifts perspective from calculated give-take to spontaneously offering from compassion. Here karma loses dichotomy of punishment and reward but transforms into the vital force which animates existence.

Chapter 1: Unraveling the Mysteries of Karma

Of all the spiritual paradigms and esoteric concepts humans have construed trying to make sense of unpredictable life events, few ideas captivate imagination as thoroughly as karma. What exactly is this invisible force that seems to maintain a ledger of rights and wrongs, dispensing consequences to beings inhabiting myriad realms across vast cycles of time? For millennia, Indian philosophies have refined sophisticated lenses to translate life's disparities through the cryptic workings of karma. Dharmic faiths uphold karma as an impersonal natural law, impartial as the law of gravity itself. As rain nourishes or erodes based solely on where it falls without concern for particular crops, karma too simply enables cycles to flow, linking intent to outcome.

Yet for most navigating karma's maze full of forks, dead-ends and shortcuts impacting known senses, there persists a sense of beguiling mystery if not bewilderment. Beyond just linking specific actions to predictable results, karma interweaves fortune and fate drawing together families, communities, collective consciousness of countries with one's solitary soul seeking significance across centuries traversed since first bursting into existence. This intricate cobweb of causal relationships spanning lifetimes reveals itself occasionally through déjà vu moments, prophetic glimpses one intuitively recognizes as having encountered somewhere before or through GE: Medium signposts guiding us gently through terrain at once familiar yet undiscovered country full of potential adventure not without its perils.

So how to make coherent sense of this esoteric paradigm that at once feels startlingly obvious yet entirely elusive! This opening chapter unravels key aspects of what karma entails alongside persistent enigmas.

The Power of Intent

Central to grasping karma is recognizing the extraordinary influence of intent, most simply put – the impulse and motivation coloring any action small or big. All major religions grapple with transmuting base greedy impulses tempting humans constantly in their untamed state. But karma philosophy goes further asserting even fleeting thoughts or unconscious speech impact tangible surroundings instantaneously in seen and unseen dimensions.

For instance Jesus proclaimed "Lustful eyes constitute adultery of the heart", a teaching echoed in other faiths extolling virtue guarding senses and purifying glance. Islam and Sikhism mandate modest dressing partly not to rouse lust. BuddhismMindfulness meditation involves witnessing thoughts non-judgmentally before skillful response emerges. Implicit across guidance is how unregulated desire creates trouble assumes wider significance when considering karmic energies constantly released through emotions, speech and gestures continue affecting people and environments long afterwards in subtle intermingling ways difficult tracing explicitly.

Here karma markedly differs say from Abrahamic notions of sin invoking morality or penance for reconciliation since True repentance holds capacity to absolve harmful actions completely as Supreme Deity intervenes with grace. Rather the operative laws governing karma resemble a metaphysical ecosystem regulated autonomously where unwholesome impulses become self-sustaining feedback loops impossible escaping through personal effort alone until requisite causes cultivated dissolving those tendencies. Think vicious cycle anger breeding hurt triggering more outrage or charitable habits reinforcing compassion fatiguelessly uplifting giver and receiver through joy's ripple effects. Significantly, while unwholesome karma gets transmitted unconsciously habitually, conscious awareness enables choice – first generating understanding then channeling intent towards ethical purpose liberates oneself, benefiting all beings automatically!.

So inescapable is intention's function within karma, it overrides external appearances to determine moral valuation. An oft cited story involves the Buddha in a past life as captain of a ship. When a man planning to murder the 500 passengers boards secretly, the captain's compassion discerns the pending disaster through meditative insight. He then skilfully steers the ship avoiding treacherous waters so all survive, thus generating great positive karma completely reversing another's ill-intent!

Ingrained habits arise from repeatedly nourished impressions. Generosity sprouts from joy in giving. Truth speaking follows ability to discern reality courageously. Leaders attuned to people's wellbeing govern with wisdom and foresight. So negative sociopolitical karma involving corruption, discrimination by race, caste, gender or disability arise from collective ignorance and fear manifesting through apathy or belief systems falsely perceived as truth. State judicial machinery unfairly incarcerating minorities also rouse outrage until reformed. Individuals cultivating mindfulness, empathy and courage reform collective destiny as new possibilities emerge..

The Ripple Effect

Karma translates loosely to action — ripples flowing with currents of intention. But it entails intricately interwoven chains enmeshing many protagonists across time and in concurrent settings. Person A's jealousy and cruelty towards B might arise from untreated childhood trauma, provoking self-loathing assumptions now mirrored outward. That hostility convincing B of innate unworthiness breeds depressive tendencies or simmering vengeance awaiting turn to inflict harm. So A's actions yield parallel suffering and dysfunction imperceptibly affecting even casual acquaintances like D who recurrently encounters troubling news til a numbing malaise sets in obscuring empathy towards victims like C who represent nameless statistics..

Ingrained social inequities often emerge camouflaged from past injustice myths once upheld as reasonable. Cultural traditions hanging on to outdated feudal mores, archaic convicted penal codes or stigma shaming queer families struggle reckoning with progressive concepts upholding constitutional rights, gender-expansive parenting and prison reforms given those born into relative privilege hesitate ceding undue advantages. Till visionary pioneers invoke radical grace dissolving barriers. Momentous collective mid-course correction then bears hope.

Individuals hold incredible leverage being single cogs turning slow gears grinding from within mammoth dehumanizing implements built thoughtlessly. Stepping off refusal to keep playing into willful blindness, cautiously reconfiguring the machine from inside, channeling resources into life-giving alternatives – seemingly small consistent actions expanding awareness that unjust systems oppose moral truth – create positive disruption. The earliest abolitionists appeared single voices easily silenced by unjust laws till daring sacrifices inspired many finding conviction carrying emancipation forward. We stand grateful inheriting hard won victories continuing to expand freedom, dignity and hope for our shared humanity. The karmic ledger favors perseverant souls seeking moral truth despite steep odds and apparent isolation.

Fate or Free Will

Perhaps no question perplexes curious minds as profoundly on matters of existence – Are lives utterly beyond control subject to arbitrary destiny or can self-determination shape one's journey? Dharmic cosmologies embrace both fate (karma phala) and self-effort (purushartha) coexisting on the soul's predestined liberation path. But distinguishing precisely between destined portions dependant on inalterable karma versus areas where current action holds full agency perplexes even discerning minds.

While material circumstances like family we are born into, socio-economic status and physical health get clearly attributed to karma portions from past lives ripening in present birth, even one's inherent nature – does one have an angry temperament or contemplative bent of mind, these too manifest due to previous conditioning. So external environmental factors and one's intrinsic psychology all constitute part of prarabdha karma – fate accruing from causes long set in motion. Interpretations differ widely on just how rigidly deterministic this inherited lot proven to be.

Yet free will has undeniable function alongside fate maps otherwise ethics become meaningless. Personal effort positively uplifts oneself and others through conscious choices cultivating wisdom, kindness, truthfulness, self-discipline with commitment to these virtues overriding inertia. Prescribed duties suiting one's life stage and station also allow fulfilling rightful purpose. Most illuminating is the role of Divine Grace blending through the juncture of fate and choice. Heartfelt surrender to the Divine has power altering preordained events drastically when cause meets supreme beneficence. Tales abound in Indic mythic epics of lost souls pivoting improbably to enlightenment through single utterances invoking sacred names that dissolve dreadful curses, heel karmic imbalances suddenly despite no tangible efforts made as Divine Grace pulls struggling souls fast forward! So fate interplays insher intricately with choice and grace on the soul's onward journey..

Types of Karma

In discussing karma, the question arises what precisely constitutes this cycle of action and consequence? Are thoughts, words and deeds weighted equally or differently? Does scale and intensity matter?

A helpful initial distinction is recognizing three kinds broadly – Prarabdha, Sanchita and Kriyaman karma spanning past, present and future. Prarabdha encompasses that portion fructifying in one's present life based on previous causes, chiefly influences visible circumstances someone is born into like parents, appearance, constitution, talents. Sanchita Karma includes the vast storehouse of all actions, reactions and residues still awaiting activation across timelines far too gargantuan tracing entirely but periodically stirring related circumstances. Kriyaman karma constitutes fresh actions we continue initiating consciously through choices encountering myriad situations, crossing paths with souls as mutual destiny unravels. So innate temperaments simultaneously intermingle destinies predetermined by cumulative latent impressions while navigating dynamics flexibly through conscious cultivation self- transforming tendencies.

Further nuanced differentiation in ancient Vedantic and Buddhist treatises analyzes precise energies bound by action-reactions. Scholarly philosophical traditions delineate complex metrics qualifying intend on, object, exertion and gain behind deeds generating karmic merits or demerits. Skillful intentions aimed at benefiting others, serving selfless duty free from selfish desire, conscious exertion guided by ethics and renouncing egoistic gain indicate superior action. Acts violating moral principles around truth, non-violence, integrity by intention, through careless effort or for gratifying desires trigger unfruitful results. Tantric and Puranic lore further distinguish between fate-altering ritual workings generating immediate fructification versus prolonged penances dissolving latent negative karma. So traditional frameworks emphasize mindful discernment regarding volition, applying effort ethically while allowing mystery of fruits unfolding gradually.

Ultimately our human scope hardly comprehends this intricate metaphysical accounting network operating simultaneously through seen and unseen vectors across space-time terrain far surpassing cognitive grasp or lifetimes spent attempting neat categorization of what ripens precisely when. Yet the grace within this cosmic riddle is how generational wisdom distills essential learning – where focus dwells, energy flows freely. By consciously channeling present actions towards wise, compassionate service, we align personal destiny to benefit all beings limitlessly through spiritual laws connecting micro to macro manifestation

Karma and Reincarnation

While karma applies universally to all actions small and mundane, its highest significance emerges in spiritual traditions accepting the doctrine of reincarnation like Dharmic faiths. Rather than just material life followed by permanent afterlife concept in Abrahamic religions, the cyclical view in Indic philosophies suggests an evolving soul presence retains causal impressions traversing across myriad lifetimes through interconnected realms subtly influencing fresh rebirths.

This allows broader perspective understanding disparities in human experience like why some people face abundant misfortune or others enjoy fortune and talents or why sociopolitical powers dominate groups arbitrarily. Karmic accumulation positive or negative transmitting across lifetimes leads to births matching those qualities. So a natural proclivity towards music or literary talents could indicate devoted practice in previous lives. Generous philanthropists inclined sharing wealth might have performed abundant charity too. But also race or disability prejudice faced by marginalized groups correlate to ignorance and structural harm inflicted historically sowing seeds now ripened through karmic action cycles.

While fatalistic resignation predestined by past karma is discouraged given each life holds opportunity for ethical development and making reparative amends, the possibilities spanning Interconnected lifetimes provides framework linking present struggles or privileges to perhaps remote causes. Most importantly the notion of rebirth until final liberative enlightenment puts moral responsibility squarely on self-development.

Across Buddhist and Hindu schools, the ultimate goal framed in various interpretations involve transcending ego-based desires perpetuating harmful ignorance. By renouncing narrow selfishness rooted in ephemeral cravings which chain consciousness to fleeting pleasures and painful clinging unable accepting life's transient impermanence, spiritual liberation gets attained. Though dialectics differ between traditions on the exact nature of what merges or quiets culminating into presence unbound by compulsions of mortal existence, the sacred duty involves consciously cultivating virtues dismantling delusions recreating vicious karmic patterns. Thus rebirth view instills profound accountability towards wise, compassionate living benefiting all beings.

Chapter 2: The Karma-Wisdom Connection

If we accept karma operates like the laws of nature executing actions and reactions precisely based on multitude minute causes, gaining wisdom involves comprehending deeper dimensions of how this intricate balance sustains the great wheel of existence in harmony.

Many philosophies conceive the universe as profoundly intentional rather than a random chaos, designed by supreme intelligence full of symbolism and purpose discoverable to the discerning eye. Dharmic cosmologies envision embedded patterns connecting microcosmic atomic arrangements, biological organic lifeforms and sweeping galactic forces carriers of ripened meaning that reveal themselves gradually through the timeless soul sojourn seeking truth. Our present life too offers indications reflecting back weighted residues from past action cycles demanding patient examination before their veil lifts ushering meaningful learning.

Where focus persists continually through habit or obsession, proportionate life-force also rings those themes repeatedly summoning attention. If consciousness dwells unaware in deep-rooted fears or aversions, situations keep manifesting close encounters foregrounding precisely those trigger points – unpleasant authority figures thwarting progress, financial instability jeopardizing security. Only upon courageously confronting embedded phobias with compassion towards ones struggling also does the cloud covering afflicted areas start dissipating because the barbed hook inside no longer needs external reference.

Similarly if arrogance fed by vanity overestimates talent blinding towards hidden flaws, humbling reversals serve harsh awakening calls. Till the instinct for self-preservation kicks in stimulated finding mentors versed traversing uneven terrain ahead who compassionately reorient stumbling ambition now ready becoming apprentice wieder than mentor prematurely.. Thus the wise embrace upticks and downturns without complaint nor boast, reading each context insightfully while flowing onwards wiser meeting life's many momentous Coyote Teacher forms!.

The Call to Awaken and Discern

If involuntarily facing recurring frustration, conflict and pain signals unchecked delusion or pride, the invitation spurring wisdom involves consciously examining where awareness needs expanding for redeeming choice to emerge. Ancient Dharmic scriptures frame the human realm among six realms of cyclical existence as that precarious middle ground between more subtle elevated planes occupied by celestial beings and democratic animal kindred downwards till purgatorial misery realms, unique position making liberation attainable through spiritual awakening seeded with discernment. For unlike ethereal beings comforted by transient enjoyment or creatures ridden by base impulses alone, humankind holds capacity glimpsing the workings of suffering alongside power to respond igniting compassionate understanding.

So the stirring call to awaken prompts any spiritual odyssey setting out sincerely seeking existential answers – Who Am I? Why is there needless tragedy and hardship interspersed amidst transcendent beauty across civilizations? Do our disparate cultures share any unifying ground despite immense diversity of symbolic expressions? What is Life whispering guiding sentient beings attempting balancing act on tightrope spanning birth and mortality without safety net except that which inner resourcefulness can summon courage grasping liberative truth?

Myriad traditions offer illuminated guideposts transmitting perennial wisdom down generations that inquiring seekers may reference realigning themselves on pathways meandering onwards. Dharmic schools propose subtly attuning through sustained practices bringing awareness in harmonious conversation with essence of reality beyond transient names-forms. Meditation dissolving ego-personas reveals witnessing presence continuous despite bodies aging. Contemplating vast interconnectedness through quantum science insights, nature's fractal symmetries or cosmic web metaphors pulls consciousness deeper respecting ephemeral forms manifesting archetypal patterns.

Where focus flows continuously through intent and effort we shape lifeworld's mirroring that quality back compelling further inquiry within. By consciously examining deluded perceptions, distorted narratives and unchecked prejudices stagnating inner vision, clarity emerges on blocade removal process. Each reclaimed awakening step strengthens discernment muscle towards that destined horizon where liberative wisdom dawns unobscured by egoism ignorance perpetuating sorrow in endless repeating cycles..

Cultivating Karma-Conscious Living

While Bodhisattva vows in Mahayana Buddhism extol aspirants to embrace voluntary rebirths selflessly guiding countless suffering beings until all attain supreme awakening, practically wisdom living unfolds fully embracing this very human birth too rarely gained. Through consciously harnessing our immense capabilities – critical inquiry challenging unjust systems, creative passions furthering cultural celebration, empathetic heart private and public dissolving barriers segregating dignity, by aligning present talents to uplifting service uncaged from narrow roles unjust social hierarchies impose, we sow merit unknowable ripples through exemplary living this remarkable opportunity offers.

The Jewish mystic tradition of Lurianic Kabbalah envisions meticulous "tikkun olam" repair principles mending tears in the great cosmic fabric caused by human failing. But implicit is acknowledging no one soul's karma-burden exists in isolation when so profoundly interdependent all destinies flow together into single confluence churning towards awakened purpose. By consciously adopting karma-aligning spiritual practices and perspectives seeking equitable community for all beings as inseparable from personal healing, we bend human civilization's unfolding more swiftly into light.

So simple everyday recurring choices like patiently hearing elderly neighbors recount here same tale finding meaningful details previously overlooked or voluntarily easing a struggling mother's burden across grocery aisles through playing joyfully with curious toddlers while she catches breath, though seemingly inconsequential actions noticing silent desperation sow little mustard seeds over lifetimes into mammoth sheltering trees offering weary wayfarers needed reprieve continuing society's long uphill journey towards compassionate justice.

The Courage to Question

Earlier when distinguishing fate versus free will, Dharmic paradigms clarify inherited karma under prarabdha influences this birth's circumstances including community and belief systems one involuntarily gets born into. But the birthright for conscious beings also gifts opportunity questioning status quo critically including outmoded unjust social structures and spiritual dogmas now needing radical revision aligned to uplift modern values like pluralism, gender rights and post-colonial hybridity. So rather than perpetrate harmful systems through inertia of privilege or survival fear, the truly wise question courageously that which conscience and reason reveals as unwholesome however normalized or sacred aura still shrouding their façade.

History honors the bold pioneer voices who awakened people out of somnolent slumber perpetrating ignorance of exclusions – whether Buddha challenging caste prohibitions barring seekers from spiritual learning or medieval mystic singers like Akka Mahadevi and Lalla Ded in Hindu Bhakti and Islamic Sufi movements advancing gender empowerment alongside their male peers as passionate spiritual exemplars. Where their profound sadhana dissolved stratified public and private barriers segregating seekers, ripples manifest centuries later through institutions led by women sages, election of empowered political leaders upholding once marginalized identities and interfaith solidarity acknowledging shared struggles.

Karma heightened through raised awareness further demands conscious examination how personal actions wittingly or discreetly continue perpetuating harm on vulnerable groups through unconsciously held privilege and micro aggressions. Well intentioned charitable organizations frequently undermine community agency imposing top down interventions without grasping systemic injustice breeding endemic poverty. Non-profit missions occasionally appropriate indigenous cultures commodifying spiritual teachings or artistic motifs insensitive towards lived heritage. Sincere atonement involves enabling space for excluded voices through restorative justice hearing, acknowledging and addressing triggered trauma before collaborative rebuilding trust. For silent tears of suffering populations carry curse fructifying through implacable karma laws that spared divinity alone transforms once ignition switch hits. But grace flows freely when vessel holds empty unleashing healing waters quenching parched lands.

By clearly illuminating ethics breaches and courageously questioning outdated feudal practices hiding behind guise of honored faiths that resist holding principle of interbeing above personal attachment to power, privilege or exclusive exceptionalism claims, we edge collectively closer upholding dignity and divinity indivisible across life.

Chapter 3: Creating Good Karma

If we imagine our actions as seeds we regularly plant in life's fertile terrain, then the fruit manifested through positive and negative karma resembles the harvest reflecting back choices made. But conditions allowing those seeds to ripen meaningfully involve appropriately nurturing the ground so skillful qualities flourish free from pesky weeds or pestilence. Ancient wisdom passed down as grandma's folklore or monastic sayings that urge carefulness what one sows intending the yield to nourish our shared community rather than greedily hoarding temporary gains heedless breeding future woe seem commonsensically sagacious.

Yet amidst loud advertisements tempting excitement through restless accumulation and disposal, the gentle farming skills tuning into natural rhythms using modest tools like our attentive hands hearts appears boringly anachronistic more suited to outdated grandparent hobbies rather than modern living expecting instant digital gratification. This chapter explores why conscious focus cultivating good karma creates joyful harvests benefitting all beings reminding that character roots nourished slowly but steadily grow mighty shade trees from tiny saplings through dedicated nurture..

NOBLE QUALITIES TO Cultivate

Philosophers analyzing mindful living seeking pathways for happiness and meaning distinguish skillful thoughts, speech and actions oriented ethically by underlying motivation. These get framed as sankaras (mental impressions), vrittis (instinctual urges) or samskaras (karmic residues) across schools coining variant terminology which generally encompass psychological tendencies manifesting outwardly molding lifeworld's through persistent application. By consciously sowing positive seeds through practicing virtues aligned to truth, compassion, integrity and wisdom traditions assure fruits from such merit (punya karma) to nourish peaceful existence naturally.

Qualities extolled ethically across cultures as character excellences or soul traits worthy striving after include:

Saucha (Purity of mind/body)

Daya (Concern for others' suffering)

Kshama (Patience with trying conditions)

Dama (Self restraint over desires)

Asteya (Honesty without stealing ideas)

Aparigraha (Simple living needs-based)

Santosha(Contentment gratitude)

Dana (Wise Generosity in need)

Dhairya (Perseverant discipline)

Other universal principles like ahimsa (non-violence), satya (truthfulness) or tapas (conscious effort) amplify these personal development practices interconnected to social reform. By training oneself consciously through litter removal volunteering, practicing receptive listening alongside sharing struggles openly or cultivating responsible digital citizenship, we begin manifesting cultural values aligned to just peaceful existence.

Mitigating Harm by Understanding Connections

When anger or outrage arises witnessing cruel injustice, wisdom involves first compassionate pause tracing systemic causes perpetuating harm before reactive words potentially escalate tensions. The quantum insight of entanglement suggests in interconnected reality, one particle influences other instantaneously at subtle planes defying physical proximity. Likewise speech carries power traversing distance barriers through invisible links manifesting outcomes aligned to their vibration. So violent language towards oppressors historically arising from legitimate trauma often breeds more brutality answering in vicious cycles. By consciously examining complex roots nurturing fear and apathy, space opens for collaborative rebuilding.

Entrepreneurial activities geared solely maximizing profits frequently encourage unethical means and ends disconnected relationships. But upon recognizing how even consumers and employees struggling faraway carry cost burden through environmental harm or labor exploitation along conveniently obscured supply chains, conscientious enterprises adopt harm mitigation practices guided by stakeholders ethic. Karma conscious businesses ensure living wages reflecting human dignity to partners throughout production cycles.

Personal habits supporting addictive substance abuse, hyper sexualized entertainment or gambling promoting greed detach awareness from damaging impacts clouding consciousness until desensitization Stage becomes new normal. Just as over farmed land depletes losing fertility through monoculture obsession, mindful moderation allows natural recovery repairing connections to essential well-being.

By uplifting ethical values honoring interdependence supporting vulnerable struggling groups through activism, mindset moves beyond reactive anger isolationism finding authentic resilience as allies. This ripens collective merit manifesting justice.

Cultivating Virtues

If immersing oneself amidst inspiring role models manifesting virtues seeking guidance to absorb elevated qualities invigorates character development, partnering intentional communities sharing sacred space sowing seeds towards similar growth intention multiplies collective merits through resonance. Monastic living traditions across faiths recognize this abundant communal fruitfulness where aspirants committed upholding vows of renunciation mutually support themselves steering all towards liberation by enveloping newcomers with patience and care while progressing in wisdom through skillful mentoring..

Often integrity habits strengthen when individuals voluntarily adopt self-regulation practices aligned to values they wish community uphold like bike commuting weekly restraining car use post-pandemic despite options or adopting pets from shelters urging others expand adoption options. Such small consistent actions tend solidarity lending momentum to larger justice issues.

By cultivating mindfulness witnessing inner reactions nonjudgmentally before response, space opens between stimuli and habitual reaction allowing pause for wiser speech. Trained discernment strengthens bonds offering better listening and counsel. So too self-examination defusing unconscious bias creates opportunities including diverse perspectives.

When media narratives stereotypically portray communities through reductive harmful norms, conscious content creators leverage storytelling craft amplifying excluded voices and projecting nuanced cultural representation advancing solidarity. Films exploring complex marginal identities with compassion seed outlooks upholding common dignity.

Through gardening metaphors, ecological thinkers frame mindful simple living practices – composting food waste for home soil enrichment, saving water through conserving baths or thoughtfully involving children planting native flower beds attracting pollinators as "cultivating virtues reconnecting our latent biophilia" – love for all life forms". Such nature aligned traditions blesses through returned abundance..

By training youth volunteering groups nurturing rescued animals, mentoring new immigrants or teaching differently abled children needed skills, generations embody empathy seeing perspectives beyond habitual notions of normal.

So everyday recurring choices create positive rippling impacts.. Karma multiplies through conscious community living guided by solidarity ethics that overcome indifference. By expanding actions from isolated self-care rituals to compassion practices alleviating neighborhood struggles, we seed flowering vines soon embracing many hearts lifting all higher.

Navigating Complex Dynamics

A woman consistently attempts unsuccessfully leaving abusive relationship because partner threatens taking custody away given her financial dependence or minimized confidence questioning judgement from longstanding emotional control. But shelter volunteers repeatedly extending support slowly nurture inner resilience as she recognizes escalating household violence scaffold patterns becoming dangerous role models absorbed by vulnerable children. As social workers diligently build case through neighborhood testimonies on her behalf petitioning courts rule emergency custody, compassionate judgment grants temporary foster home stability, restraining authority halting toxic exposure.

In this complex situation where victim faces manipulative threats and actresses violence losing tempers through reactionary anger, multiple causes interplay. But collective merit emerged as outsider allies reinforced self-worth and safety instincts fueling her departure. By granting grace aligning best interests compassionately rather than perpetuating volatile dynamics through polarized judgment, intervention shifts destiny positively.

A corrupt bureaucrat amasses properties through years exploiting legal loopholes seemingly immune courting power brokers guaranteeing protection till courageous whistleblowers daringly leak confidential dealings to free press. Investigative reporters lines connect illicit deals immediately dismantling significant portfolio overnight when public outrage peaks global diaspora advocacy flooding concerned minister's ears as erstwhile foreign policy allies also pull out associated investments ashamed by ethical violations..

By persistently upholding dharma principles truth and justice despite steep odds change ripens suddenly as oppressive edifices built by brute power quickly weaken when opaque veils lift revealing festering wounds spurring legal accountability and truth commissions urging reform...

So in manifold situations we traverse masterfully or stumble through daily, collective merit manifests elevating problem-solving beyond reactionary anger by upholding ethical wisdom compassionately applied towards restoring justice particular scenarios cry for... Through karma philosophy lens, complex dynamics involve multifaceted previously built environments, personal temperaments cultured unconsciously overtime and fresh latent tendencies awakening together influencing outcomes in context. By consciously examining our own social placements built on historic privilege plus places vulnerability still needing mature insight, we hold space also hearing those deprived by status quo allowing empathy guide appropriate intervention response alignments best interests while being guidingly firm stopping further harm. This ripens unity federating allies towards common uplifting goals..

Conclusion

Karma as conceived across eastern spiritual traditions frames a lens understanding life's often bewildering complexities simply through action-reaction phenomenology yet its intricacies encompass collective dynamics across vast interdependent chains spanning beyond isolated events or individual control. By consciously examining motive and consequences, speech and behaviors can align to ethical living growing peace and justice.

The Role of Intention

Karma theory emphasizes volition and motivation driving actions over outward appearances. This internal compass steers external acts either upholding ethical ideals or violating moral principles. A helpful framework distinguishing skillful from unskillful intentions (cetana) emphasizes four key reference points:

1. Renunciation – curbing selfish desires distorting wisdom

2. Goodwill – cultivating concern for others' welfare

3. Harmlessness – compassionate commitment to non-violence

4. Equanimity – upholding dignity across all beings

When personal decisions get guided consciously by these four cardinal orientations, actions generated lead to merits benefitting self and others. Often unconscious habit patterns chain behaviors blindly without connecting to harmful impacts on vulnerable populations and environments. By pausing to examine motives through questioning filters if outcomes improve equity and justice for underprivileged while mitigating harm on ecosystems, intention realigns to mindfulness.

Courageous self-regulation resisting internal urges counter to ethical principles represents important milestone as character gets shaped by integrity. Social psychology experiments have consistently shown situational peer pressure easily sways individual behaviors against better judgment. By consciously examining motives and conduct in light of potential harm, conscience steers actions well.

The Social Web of Merit

While Balinese Hinduism's concept of Karma Phala mirrors cosmos maintaining harmony through moral equilibrium of deeds ripening good or bad fruits precisely, Buddhist perspectives recognize more complex collective conditions allowing results to manifest. So a child's loving nurture arise through parents, teachers and supportive village networks together enabling healthy development beyond isolated effort. By considering interconnected debts owed living interdependently, humility arises.

Gratitude practices give structure appreciating how others' struggle uplifted progress or how common inheritance like safe nature, public roads and national security manifest through shared citizenship beyond selfish efforts. Seeing interbeing of shared destiny cultivates deep reverence for all constituent elements miraculously synchronizing behind veil of mundane ordinariness.

Even simplistic spiritual solo practices like ritual flower offerings or volunteering involve many seen and unseen contributors whose ripe fruits sustain practice. The industrious bee gathering pollen aerating soil, organic farmers protecting biodiversity refraining pesticides, floral vendors forgoing holidays, cataloguers ensuring ethical fair-trade symbol etc together enable virtual act of offering blossoms manifesting devotion linked through compassionate marketplaces.

By consciously expanding identity boundaries beyond isolated self-referencing, we inhabit the Anthropocene era's challenges as collective ecological karma calling for collaborative redress no longer escapable through individual ascendance or siloed nation building alone but interconnected redemption all beings imperiled by climate catastrophes collectively face. So universal ethics seeking collective merits aligning to social and restorative justice brings hope.

Cultivating Merit through Service

Selfless service offered sincerely to benefit common wellbeing untainted by selfish motives of public recognition or transactional tit-for-tat calculations bears manifold fruits as community resilience and harmony get strengthened. Humble civic efforts supporting local food pantries, volunteering weekend elderly care or mentoring disadvantaged youth might seem modest contributions on surface. But unquantifiable merits ripple widely through qualitative bonds nurturing solidarity.

Caregivers working compassionately alongside marginalized groups by uplifting agency and capacities rather than rushed transactional charity nourish deeper roots so communities blossom freely. The fruits of service arise from empowering relationships that dismantle limiting social hierarchies steeped in paternalism, savior mentalities or ableist assumptions of normalcy. By truly seeing and addressing structural violence denying opportunities that policy exclusion breeds, transformation gets centered around those whose dignity was denied rather than publicity chasing allies.

Eco-spiritual movements thoughtfully involving indigenous earth wisdom traditions alongside intersectional ecofeminist, queer and critical race lenses offers inclusive environmentalism that heals by acknowledging historic harms perpetuated through conservation colonialism. Broad participatory ethics seeking restorative justice brings humility correcting blindspots.Thus service cultivated self-reflectively lays foundations based on solidarity and trust from which local resilience blooms perennially paying gratitude forward..

By consciously examining privilege and cultural assumptions carried unconsciously even within well-intentioned charitable interventions, space allows upholding deep listening guiding reciprocal transformation rather than superficial reform alone. This spiritual deepening SERVICE that opens possibilities rewriting future history.

LIFE UNFOLDING THROUGH the lens of karma offers a framework making sense of personal ups and downs by tying individual moral development to collective living. By understanding key drivers of actions as skillful versus unskillful intentions, we gain leverage consciously cultivating positive sankharas aligned to truth, compassion and justice while dissolving those rooted in harmful ignorance and prejudice. Seeing oneself interdependently connected to social webs of supportive causes for personal growth and accomplishments breeds humility. It inspires paying forward merit. The fruits of good karma arise from empowering others through conscious service versus self-centered accumulation. By dismantling unjust systems and hierarchies steeped in historic oppression, liberation blooms for all.

Chapter 4: Living Out Karma in Daily Life

Living Out Karma in Daily Life

Beyond lofty spiritual goals of ending karmic cycles, wisdom teachings stress putting principles immediately into practice through conscious choices we face routinely that either compound problems or cultivate solutions. Our homes, workplaces, friend circles and neighborhoods offer fertile ground implementing karma philosophies practically.

Karma in Relationships

Family life furnishes first lessons in sowing harmony or discord through speech and actions that affectionately nourish bonds or reactively strain ties over time. When exhausted parents implement screen restrictions, thoughtful dialogue explaining reasons avoids authoritarian force alone intimacy preserving. Entreating cooperation through consistent incentives outlasts scolding distrusting independence kids clamor. Loving speech manifests returning empathy.

Romantic partnerships thrive when both nurture mutual understanding respecting boundaries authentically caring, not possessive control-driven demands expecting happiness derived through another. Generosity nourishing joy uncoerced builds resilient reliance weathering external storms together. Ripening authentic intimacy fragrantly through seasons harvesting lasting fulfillment as each boldly fertilizes common field, not isolated plots separately hoarded.

Cordial professional relationships unlock collaborative performance surpassing lone achievers when diverse thinkers brainstorm openly. Appreciating unique strengths aligns projects smoothly. Even conflict borne policies securing justice when leaders exercise democratic patience forging compromising wisdom mutually palatable. Providing disagreement room for expression weaves cohesive team spirit.

Across cases, applying karma lens reveals how consciously transforming reactive impulse into compassionate response sows ripples uplifting relationships to mutuality. Patience is key ingredient ensuring empathy space to work wonders.

Karma in Workplaces

Beyond chasing career status tethering identity security, mindful jobs sustain passion purpose promoting social impacts while supporting livelihood reasonably. When organizations implementing restorative practices reduce employee turnover through uplifting workplace culture beyond punishing policies alone, wisdom manifests valuing all contributors.

Leaders seeking common prosperity address historic pay discrimination respecting labor rights, thereby seeding win-win motivational climate benefitting diverse stakeholders fairly. Mindsets that simply maximize profits frequently externalize environmental costs upon common assets air, water, forests reaching tragedy of erosion cliffs where none wins. But reforming frameworks to honor ecological integrity, just access alongside returns rejuvenates enterprises resiliently.

When bosses mentoring staff nurture talents patiently through upskilling support, employee retention results reward training investments further attracting loyal competence. Work designed cooperatively embracing automation revolution can liberate human potential from repetitive jobs towards more meaningful service. By consulting cultural wisdom keepers, restoring land stewardships and uplifting marginalized genius, green innovation bears sustainable fruits.

Applying karma lens at organizational levels reveals that valuing people, planet and ethical prosperity together manifests conscientious capitalism where all boats rise rather than winner take all modalities amplifying inequality gaps now urgently needing upliftment.

Karma in Communities

Neighborhood living shares public goods, so cooperative actions enhance quality of life – organizing rotating night patrols protecting vulnerable elders, hosting intercultural block parties for cross-pollinating solidarity, mobilizing resident interest lobbying governments to upgrade neglected spaces.

When marginalized castes face barriers due to ingrained stigma, pioneering residents voluntarily inviting, hiring and celebrating cultural gifts offered builds interdependent harmony. Rippling stories of compassion dissolving distrust spreads hope.

Urban farming communal plots foster ecological integrity across generations and demographics nurturing community resilience through native vegetation supporting pollinators, composting networks closing local waste loops sustainably alongside public Rainwater harvesting convergence carving scarcity into abundant prosperity manifesting health, beauty and festivity.

Applying karma lens to shared habitats reinforces how inclusive policies uplifting minority subgroups together remedy structural violence. Crown jewels of civilization shine upholding justice, as heroic leaders testify.

Karma in Environment

Seeing humanity as gardeners tasked stewarding green domains sustaining all creatures great and small instills accountability within lifestyles, policies and economic frameworks to uphold ecology of life. Where relentless land exploitation threatens indigenous sacred sites or industrial human camps expand callously driving other beings extinct through collapsing biodiversity, negative karma accrues violently denying interdependent harmony.

But green communities guided by biomimetic principles linking buildings through edible forest networks filled abundantly through seasonal harvest celebrations build habitats where humans, plants and wildlife all thrive together resiliently. When green spaces become inclusivemulti-functional hubs for families relaxing, children playing naturally, teenagers exchanging ideas, adults learning reskilling trades based on peer tutoring, elderly imparting cultural heritage through intergenerational storytelling; public parks manifest civilizational apex as cultural crossroads community oases!

Applying karma lens to lifestyles dependent upon fossil fuel luxury directly exported from frontline forests bearing climate impacts makes visible co-creation of cycles jeopardizing poor disproportionately. But transition pathways to curb emissions through clean energy targets and circular economies together offer hope writing future history where economic priorities realign serving to uplift people and planet simultaneously rather than short-term profits alone.

BY APPLYING SPIRITUAL principles of karma consciously through everyday lifestyle, vocational and public policy spheres, the deep insights of wisdom teachings translate into practical justice, ecological harmony and cooperative uplifting of our shared destinies. Simple conscious choices compound positively when priorities get structured around compassion and mindfulness of karmic ripples spawned beyond isolated cost-benefit calculations. By uplifting those struggling at margins directly into positions of dignified interdependence and participatory leadership, society transforms towards resilient abundance available for all global households where none get excluded any longer.

Karma in Self-Development

On the inner journey towards wisdom and purpose, karma perspective offers reflective framework making sense of personal highs and lows spiritually.

Why me? Mystery of destiny

When facing intense life struggles despite sincere ethics, self-pity inflames suffering further alienating reality. By accepting prarabdha this moment ripened through complex causality beyond current control, while focusing self-determined agency changing course ahead, insight dawns uplifting many stuck similarly. Things happen not only to us but also for us to become wiser.

Patience, the fruit ripens in time

Natural fruits manifest gradually through seasonality; so too karmic seeds sown require gestation before visible shoots. Premature picking spoils essential maturation. Through patient perseverance holding faith purpose underpins apparent chaos, triumph of spirit awaits beyond next bend inevitably.. Timing flows aligned to rhythms larger than selves.

Courage, growth means leaving shells behind

The heaviness felt in anxieties rooting uncertainty about unsteady futures often encapsulates profound opportunity for enlarging identity constructs built earlier now turned restrictive. Like the mother bird nudging fledglings to fly or ocean waves relentless eroding rigidity land into before flowing onwards, grace abides when fears faced unclench grasping false securities outgrown.

By affirming larger truth dwelling beyond absence alone, wings meant lifting worldviews expand gradually vision dissolving imaginary limitations once boundaries defining self concepts exceeded boldly.

Karma in Managing Emotions

Habitual reactions rooted in anger, envy or prejudice often perpetuate friction eclipsing wisdom. By pausing without suppression to reflect mindfully on feelings arising before responding, space allows recognizing where unprocessed pain might need care before projecting outward. Maintaining meditative practice strengthens equanimity enduring life's ups and downs.

Karma in Facing Hardships

When enduring aridity periods emotionally or scarcity facing economically, resilience strengthens prudently consolidating essentials appreciating interdependence. During night tunnels when light fades futility threatens faith, inhabiting darkness courageously often ripens spiritual dawn nearest. Like compost waste nourishing garden blooms or Katydids hymn announcing monsoon blessings, grace works alchemically through life's churning phases.

Karma in Making Amends

Relationships frequently fracture when harmful actions seeming innocuous widen rifts through dismissal avoiding responsibility. Mustering courage after festering quiet to initiate reconciliation dialogue assuming humility ownership without defensiveness manifests mutual healing restoring bonds wiser having navigated breach.

Karma in Being Inspired

The lotus lifting pristinely unblemished petals above murky waters symbolizes spiritual wisdom manifesting suddenly midst mundane routine through grace alighting passion reigniting meaning or synchronicities weaving coherence feeling fate's hand upholding higher vision. When momentum lifts transcending self, destiny enters positively as self-concepts expand..

Karma Case Studies in Everyday Dilemmas

Workplace Conflict

Scenario: A startup's overworked engineer experiences burnout causing missed deadlines. Her manager worries about launch delays and angrily threatens job loss rather than addressing wellbeing. Communication breaks down worsening tensions.

Karma Perspectives: By pausing without escalating reactions, compassionately evaluate multiple causes – unreasonable work expectations, mental health stigma, lack of team support resources. Practice non-judgment listening to understand all views. Cooperatively implement solutions valuing staff welfare alongside organizational needs.

Outcomes: Creating open channels for ethical feedback without retaliation builds trust and collective responsibility. Supporting healthy work-life balance sustains careers and performance long-term.

Family Estrangement

Scenario: A youth feels unfairly treated by strict parental controls and leaves home abruptly after a bad argument without reconciling. Years later both regret the prolonged silence.

Karma Perspectives: Recall the anxiety of young adulthood seeking independence. How might sheltered upbringings limit communicating needs? With time, accept mutual fallibility. Now respectfully reconnect by naming impacts of actions without accusations.

Outcomes: Owning one's part in family breakdowns allows maturity making amends. Healing past scars nurtures future bonding. Forgiveness dissolves stubborn pride.

Karma Exercises for Everyday Ethics

Beyond lofty spiritual goals, karma principles applied routinely build wisdom incrementally through examining day-to-day thoughts, speech and actions. These exercises offer practical guidance along the path.

Speech and Relationship Karma

Notice communication dynamics when interacting with varied personalities without bias. What underlying needs or insecurities interact within confrontational conversations that escalate tensions? How might listening without interruption or asking thoughtful questions dispel misunderstanding?

Imagine two long estranged friends, childhood bonds now distant through years of silence. Draft a reconciliation message honestly owning your part without bitterness. Offer invitation for dialogue rebuilding trust.

Witness daily speech habits over one week. Reflect if any gossip tendencies manifest judging others' reputation without consent. Consider ripple harms caused maligning individuals versus speaking directly with compassion.

Action and Work Karma

Recall work scenario where leadership decisions affected many stakeholders beyond self. Analyze considerations that determined outcomes balancing complex interests. In hindsight, what alternative actions may have upheld dignity and ethics equally for all groups impacted?

Reimagine capitalist assumptions purely maximizing Shareholder profits measuring narrow financial indicators alone. If prioritizing humanitarian and ecological metrics equally beyond quarters growth, how might decision-making shift towards inclusive holistic models?

When noticing anxiety around job uncertainty, investigate underlying self-concepts threatened. Beyond wanting workplace stability, what parts of identity attach to professional status needing reassurance? Consider what anchors self-worth if credentials, roles and praise fade.

Habit and Emotion Karma

When addictive behavior patterns chain consciousness narrowing destructive feedback cycles of craving, gratification and withdrawal, how might pausing to assess root insecurities help reclaim agency? Consider supports needed for creating emotional and physical space interrupting impulsive urges.

For a recurring emotional trigger causing regular overreactions, track associated minimization, projection and repression habits distancing vulnerability during the building episode. Then journal authentic uncensored feelings surfacing without self-blame. Notice Moving through the full experience releases pent-up energy; what clarity follows for resolving intensity?

During upcoming family holiday gatherings often bringing anxiety or loneliness, plan rhythm of private reflection time alongside togetherness nourishing introvert and extrovert needs. Savor solitude balancing external emotional demands avoiding earlier holiday burnout. Spending time in nature or expressing creativity works well too.

Identity and Privilege Karma

Notice any visible identity markers granting social privileges unfairly elevating access and credibility conferred by default without personal merit – race, upbringing prestige, gender expression etc. Then consciously cultivate ally ship uplifting colleagues who contribute comparable talents yet navigating systemic biases limiting deserved success.

For a marginalized group facing oppression amplified in recent news, analyze historical beliefs and governance policies perpetuating societal inequities generationsally. Consider what everyday speech, consumption habits or social unawareness sustain ignorance upholds status quo indirectly. Then state action intention cultivating consciousness that educates self on blind spots.

Living Out Karma Consciously

Exploring how the principle of karma manifests visibly in relationships, workplaces and systemic issues reveals sophistication behind simplistic cultural shorthand of "what goes around comes around".

The cycles of ethical cause and effect have profound impacts rippling across unseen interconnections tying humanity together in an intricate web of being. Yet within these binding constraints also lies radical freedom. Every small choice sowing peace or discord becomes incredibly consequential.

Progress unfolds gradually through cumulative actions. As visionary leader Tarun Cherian reflected during India's arduous freedom struggle – "When millions begin doing little things with love, they embody a silent spiritual evolution embroidering another history."

The practice of witnessing thoughts and emotions mindfully allows responding with wisdom rather than reacting blindly across tangled situations. Regular reflection nurtures this muscle strengthening equanimity amidst life's ups and down.

By consciously examining beliefs, habits and privileges perpetuating harmful ignorance and indifference, space opens for accountability and restorative change. Where focus flows continuously, energetic patterns manifest. Shifting attention towards justice and renewal fuels external momentum.

While destiny has unknown dimensions beyond control, present voluntary actions assert self-determinism ripening circumstances differently. By understanding behavioral Karma with Msg managing work stresses or family dynamics, significant outcomes follow too. Conscious choice fuels trajectories.

Through everyday mindfulness examining roots of speech and action while nurturing virtues like courage, empathy and integrity, ripples of karma align increasingly to wisdom and compassion manifesting social uplifting.

Chapter 5 : freedom
from karma

Transcending Karma's Web

Karma theories ubiquitous across Eastern faiths pinpoint root causes of sorrow and suffering arising from ignorance of interdependence and impermanent nature of phenomena as constantly arising and dissolving. By clinging after ephemeral pleasures hoping to grasp lasting happiness externally or rejecting painful circumstances through aggression and avoidance, deluded consciousness darts between anxiety and anguish unable to internally access peaceful equanimity abiding deeper behind life's passing ups and downs.

Attachments to social identities, wealth and accomplishments as perpetual security buffers against mortality also chain awareness ignorantly across realms of becoming, ever wanting without lasting fulfillment since nothing grasped retains immutable essence.

Thus the keen insight offered philosophically regarding human dilemma is two fold — perceiving fleeting surface play of forms with non-attached equanimity and cultivating penetrating inquiry interrogating falsely stabilized perceptions of fixed separate self or external locality harbouring freedom. This profound internal shift from renting condominiums within cosmos to recognizing oneself as conscious ground housing passing experiences liberates seeking from slaves becoming to joyous beings consciously creating.

By renouncing narrow identities tethering awareness to particular accumulating personal ambitions and dissolving prejudice demarcating imaginary cleavages across communities, emergence of awakening heralds — impartial spacious presence abiding at ease viewfully beyond subject-object fragmentation. No longer captive worshipper kneeling before conceptual altars. Rather the ultimate seer whose unveiled sight basks through myriad forms, the eternal light animating all bodies cosmic with equal grace, great liberator whose fearless wisdom guides innumerable beings journeying across stormy bhavasagar oceans to shore.

Witnessing Practice for Non-Attachment

Regular meditative practice provides systematic methodology training faculties steadying wayward awareness continually appropriating momentary phenomena for bolstering egocentric cravings resisting loss through grasping or aversion. By intentionally fixing observing gaze at ephemeral arising's — physical sensations, emotional turbulence, compulsive thinking routines — while relinquishing reflexive urge to indulge phenomena for entertainment, sustenance or profit, mental muscle strengthens simply abiding amidst passing displays without destabilization each dissolution brings thought addicted minds.

Just as mountain peak remains unmoved glorious through seasons while clothing appearances change or mighty oak firm rooted through gale stands while fallen leaves scatter, witnessing presence gradually awakens abiding true essence unchanged behind manifestations. Freed thus from compulsions chasing or rejecting experiences that chain mortal minds swinging perpetually between anxiety and anguish, profound peace dawns abiding timeless.

When attention no longer diverts habitually towards gratifying impulses but turns inquisitively tracing transient forms to very edge of arising, crafted illusion of continuity collapses revealing empty essence and dependent origination of all phenomena. Like phantom snake conjured alarm that disappears under light examining rope, so too conceptual bonds loosen freeing awareness towards open clarity beyond mental prisons.

Understanding the Social Construction of Identity Concepts

If meditative insight deconstructs psychological tendencies projecting imagined continuity onto experiences, complementary intellectual inquiry examines how popular narratives mythical, religious propound notions "individual self" substantial enduring entity progressing linearly across lifetime through chronological phases making coherent personality essence carried immutable lifetimes regardless contexts, communities colouring consciousness critically. Philosophers term this assumed separate self possessing fixed attributes over time as "essentialist identity" construing personal viability through origin stories privileging certain signified biological aspects while obscuring intersectional facets shaping complex subjectivity through dynamic eco-social contexts perpetually interacting, evolving.

Post-structural analysis reveals even gender, ableist or ethnic categorizations enshrined institutionally that determine access to resources, opportunities and dignity arbitrarily based on birth happenstance beyond individual control emerge through fluid subjectifying sociocultural ascriptions perpetually contested and co-created between structures exerting hegemonic domination versus communities reclaiming self-authored agency through everyday negotiations and resistance politics.

So rational examination exposes how conditioned fetishizing group traits, birthmarks or other qualifiers arrogantly estranges interconnected existence into fragmented camps competing entitled rights, blinded towards the interbeing of all expressions constituting the shared field of conscious play. No phenomena manifest independently essential by own accord but interdepend dependently arising mutually supported by multitude causes and conditions within vast web of intercausal relationships.

By consciously inspecting essentialist notions carried culturally across history powerfully shaping social attitudes and allocated privileges, humility arises seeing through accidental identities invested for bolstering insecure egos defending status against loss through age, infirmity or external threats beyond control. Equanimity blossoms accepting all transient forms manifested the shining mirror of awareness without prejudice. Renouncing egoistic notions "my pain, my history, my deprivations above others" allows upholding dignity and hope for all beings equally. For in the deepest reality nothing gets excluded from compassionate concern..

Practicing Socially Engaged Spirituality

While profound stages turning inward definitely uplift clarity and empathy furthering personal maturation eventually benefitting society indirectly through exemplary conduct transmitting wisdom legacy across generations, urgent existential crises facing interconnected global civilisation today — climate emergency, biodiversity collapse and rising nationalist authoritarianism threaten civilizational viability more immanently demanding compassion into radical collective action addressing present ground realities, dismantling unjust systems and healing historic exclusions.

Here revolutionary teachings like Buddha's four noble truths diagnosing the omnipresent reality of suffering, insightful grasp of its sociocultural origins, cessation through non-attached equanimity and mindfully compassionate eightfold path gain timely relevance as frameworks making conscious well-reasoned choices what role one plays breaking oppressive cycles —

Are my lifestyle habits and privileges consciously examined dumping undue climate burdens exterior by outsourcing carbon emissions and deforesting across invisible obscured supply chains upon poor indigenous forest communities who contributed least fossil fuel usage?

Does partisan news media consumed perpetuate dangerous prejudice through propaganda caricaturing marginalised minorities as threats, drowning their vulnerable voices pleading for empathetic inclusion and reconciliatory justice?

Do investments fund military industrial complexes financially incentivising cycles of fear and domination or ethical enterprises grounded serving community resilience?

While intensive spiritual praxis strengthens resilient clarity to endure unpredictable challenges ahead with courage, insight further demands uplifting outcast and afflicted populations through engaged activism, lending privilege and platforms furthering systemic healing. For the inner light integrating shadow also kindles radiance for illuminating collective liberation..

Deathless Enlightenment Transcending Karma

While virtuous application manifesting wisdom and compassion bear fruits gradually uplifting communities karmically in greater cycles of harmony, the eastern nondual traditions grandly herald possibility of profound metaphysical liberation named variously across schools — moksha, bodhi, kaivalya, nirvana — attained when through lifetimes of conscious exertion and service, affinity with mystical grace matures rending veils of illusion completely. The awakened state realises one's deathless luminous essence abiding eternal beyond corporeal dissolution or phenomenal becoming.

Depicted intricately through symbolism of Padmasambhava's five wisdoms in Tibetan Buddhism, Shiva's ecstatic tantric dance resonating between cemetery grounds and Himalayan peaks or Dakshinamurty legend in Advaita illustrating primordial guru first initiating self-inquiry outside constructs of language, generations of sages sing inspired envisioning the ineffable expanse dawning once consciousness sheds last residue of separate self-sense. All violent dialectics repose embraced equally into nondual equanimity beyond fathoming thought corrupted by dualistic habits. Sarvam Khalvidam Brahma resonates the upanishad mahavakyas Everything is Brahman the absolute plenum grounding manifold appearance

While most householders aspire gradually progressing to more subtle planes through self purification practices seeking fortunate rebirth consolations, these rare deathless heights ever beckon the daring ones renouncing regulated social matrices to abandon everything for irrevocable liberation in this very birth!

Chapter 6: The Twelve Laws of Karma

Beyond the common cultural shorthand that "what goes around comes around", the sophisticated doctrine of karma operates through twelve precise universal laws woven subtly into reality's dynamic fabric spanning seen and unseen dimensions. By comprehending key principles governing how volitional action Initiates causality translating into appropriate effects, we gain liberating wisdom navigating life's fortunes skillfully as conscious co-creators rather than fatalistically as helpless victims buffeted unpredictably by random chance.

The Law of Creation

"Yathaa Krathu, Thathaa Bhava" – As one acts, so one becomes" – Thus opens first Karmic Law stating we actively compose lifeworld's aligning to predominant qualities cultivated consciously. Of numerous forces influencing existence, intentional choice retains freedom modifying destiny's direction. Developing virtues manifest positive conditions.

The Law of Humility

Facing favorable fortunes, humility stays cautious not taking undue credit claiming glory swelled through self-pride alone nor judging others' plight arrogantly assuming responsibility faults entirely their own. For Intricate networks of visible and subtle causes converge rippling benevolence before one surrounded fortuitously by kind souls, timely opportunities and buoyant health. Tides lift all ships synchronously as befits seasons. Staying humble allows wisely channeling blessings further.

The Law of Growth

When enduring adversity courageously, one evolves through ordeals necessary facilitatIng wisdom impossible accessing living comforted complacency. Gold repeatedly burns emerging purified, lotuses uplift pristine above muddy waters. Tests determine sincere seekers committing spiritual service from selfish converts hoping parley piety into profitable privileges. Surrendered souls accept destiny gratefully despite mysterious ups and downs which strengthen surrender.

The Law of Responsibility

While fate's unseen hand steers circumstances unfathomable, radical freedom rests responding consciously. Traversing challenges Illegitimately faced due to oppressive systemic inequities traces to collective karma accrued historically. Though unjustly born disprivileged by virtue of race, gender or disability unfavorably, resigned bitterness keeps one shackled awaiting external intervention alone. Seizing responsibility where possible through disciplined effort and skillful means manifests liberation gradually where structural barriers shift expand.

The Law of Connection

No being exists isolated solely responsible for success attained individually. Network Invisible through subtle realms channels opportunities, relationships and resources culminating visible attainments. By recognizing humble debts owed constantly to family patrons, faceless farmers and risk-taking investors in collective interdependence all ripening fruits through cooperation,

wisdom dawns transcendIng narcissist ego towards hospitality
mentoring all to rise together.

The Law of Focus

The trajectory of awareness fuels life paths – anxiety meanders indecisively while ambition propels efficiently. By intentionally directing attention consistently towards ethical actions without wavering or digressing expediently for gratifying desires against conscience, concentration manifests destiny decisively. Distracted minds breed carelessness losing wealth, health and wisdom. But focused living upholds priorities most sacred with fullest integrity despite conflicting demands.

The Law of Giving and Hospitality

When resources gathered through diligence and fortune get shared generously without seeking recognition but uplifting common dignity, abundance multiplies beyond selfish hoarders tallying exchange ledgers rigidly. Karma ripens from selfless caring intention, not quantified fruits reaped. By unconditionally welcoming strangers warmed with compassion trusting our shared divinity Implicitly seeds ripening community receiving all inhabitants as kin without barriers.

The Law of Here and Now

Drinking joyously this moment's nectar remains thirst quenched unlike chasing envisioned scenarios for future fulfillment once conditions hopefully Improve. Gladdening present builds equanimity greeting unknowable next phases with faith earned through perseverance. Neither mourning problems Inherited nor fantasizing salvation but boldly wading reality with firm kindness fully awakens.

The Law of Change

Since no moment abides permanently without flux, rather than chaining identity attachments hoping to stabilize permanence externally, radical wisdom accepts lovingly all transformations life's seasons cyclic brings appreciating being's opportunity through Incarnating temporary human forms. Pining perpetuates suffering. Flowing without clinging allows savoring experiencees peacefully even departing death of forms when consciousness merges back home. Impermanence permits renewal.

The Law of Patience and Reward

No seed sprouts Instantly but incubates until conditions ripe. Karma fructifies aligned to perfect rhythms exceeding impatient demands or doubts by not manifesting visibly. Through unwavering faith upheld despite externally missing evidence, greater glories arrive unexpectedly. Divine timing fulfills graciously In right hour all who persist faithfully without wavering drooping spirit.

The Law of Significance and Inspiration

Intuition glimpsing meaningful patterns and guiding synchronicities unexpectedly helps navigate uncertainty.inspired when aligning petty actions trustingly to self-transcending service. Mingling sacred and mundane no longer through consecrated rituals alone butsurfing elevated meaning right where one stands uplifts spiritual posture beyond drudgery. Signs give way where .significance elevates existence

The Law of Conservation

While ephemeral forms fade, Invisible essence endures indestructible reality ever awaits rediscovery behind mask Maya dons. No sincere seeking nor tears shed requesting divine audience drops vain Into abyss without cosmic registering. Trust life's larger logistics upholding justice and meaning despite outward chaos.

..Faith bridges all losses love sustained cannot fill eventually By assimilating laws mapping subtle territory where karma engenders, consciousness grasps liberating wisdom guiding destiny with astute graciousness necessary building peaceful enlightened ..societies

Chapter 7: The Law of Creation

In spiritual wisdom traditions across cultures, the central teaching that each individual or collective co-authors destiny through exercised choices profoundly empowers radical responsibility towards shaping life consciously rather than resignation blaming external forces.

The first cardinal Law of Karma expounds this active participation declaring "Yathaa Krathu, Thathaa Bhava (As one acts, so one becomes)". Daily thoughts, speech and deeds channel potent creative energies birthing corresponding life-worlds which reflect back those predominant qualities through multifaceted visible results and subtle influences.

So the mindful ones desiring peace or prosperity sow its causes by thinking, speaking and committing actions suffused through masterful diligence rather than anxious speculation. By focusing patiently, destiny blooms gradually as orchard trees first nurtured to bear sweet fruits in due season.

The Power of Thought

Far from random, the vast causal nexuses giving rise spatio-temporal reality remarkably resembles the embedded architectures mirroring consciousness. When habitual thoughts flow uncontrolled towards pessimism dragging moods through draining swamps, multiplying misfortunes appear confirming unconscious prophecies.

But uplifted spirits basking gratitude pave fortunes ahead attracting grace. Resilience visualized burgeons inner resources overcoming hurdles once deemed unsurpassable. Athletes clarify self-concepts mentally rehearsing glories tasted through disciplined collective actualization. Doubt yielding to dedicated practice earns laurels. Where mind goes, energy flows forth impacting the field of possibilities decisively.

The Dance of Words

"Vāgartaṃ karma" meaning speech acts creatively, expound ancient Indian wisdom teachings revealing subtle potency words unleash qualifying emergent reality incrementally overtime. Soothing affectionate words awaken talents accelerating destinies once adrift rescued into purposefulness. Childhood cruelties haunting beyond years impede actualization until compassion dissolves hurt. Diplomatic dialogue sustains peace while deceit sows warfare. Impassioned oratory transformed destinies of communities. Words spoken carries secrets shaping worlds. Discerning speech building trust seed cooperative unfolding. Mysterious are karmic fruits ripening from tongues uncontrolled reacting habitually. Conscious choice harnesses power.

Participating Co-Creation

While cosmic consciousness births myriad forms through inscrutable will, direct participation carves particular crystallizations from infinite potentialities awaiting activation. The sculptor's chisel clearing specific elegant statuary lying obscured within coarse matter applies metaphorically. Channeled through biological faculties constraining yet the timeless soul sojourn retains relative freedom partially coloring passages unpredictably.

So too while macro environments like hereditary characteristics, embedding cultures and socioeconomic placements constitute prarabdha fate-karma proportions conditioning this lifetime's trajectory considerably, phala fruitions from active programming using present scope for upliftment allows some rewriting of destinies. Reformers have catalyzed revolutionary leaps transcending previous limiting boundaries dramatically through perseverant choices despite steep odds confronting initially. Conscious living harmonizes fate and freewill gracefully.

Cultivating Conscious Creation

If truly comprehending life as active co-creation by participating agents rather than happenstance of randomness breeding anxiety surrendering control, profound urgency awakens steering each thought, word and action intentionally towards ethical ends. Personal habits nourishing spiritual growth align gradually uplifting larger communities through conscious responsibility.

Taming Desires

Habitual reactions indulge immediate gratification even violating principles. Repeated yielding gradually strengthens temptation's magnetism until consequences faced staring bleakly. By pausing pleasure seeking long enough examining compulsions objectively, space opens reconsidering are dominant motivations wisely aligned. Do pursuit of promotions and pay alone grant meaningful success when bartering family intimacy or health priorities? When renown chases fame ruthlessly, credibility often suffers precisely. What enduring seeds sprout through fleeting virtual distractions? Where attention is invested substantially shapes realities harvest eventually.

SEEKING HIGHER COUNSEL

Navigating adversities often requires insight exceeding habitual capacities. Through humility seeking guidance from life's wounded healers who transformed personal traumas into wisdom assets uplifting society, perspective expands as higher reasoning filters difficulties in alternate light. The survivor's resilience carries teachings more potent than untested gurus offering superficial platitudes alone.such role models kindle hope. Tempered mentors administer realities' bitter medicine insightfully awakening one to glory glimpsed accepting limitations courageously first.

Speech Mindfully Seasoned

When impatience breeds reactionary outbursts defensively before we investigate trigger issues calmer or petulant blame projecting failure unpleasantly arise, contemplative efforts pausing deeply why particular situations recurrently evoke such patterns reveal much. Perhaps harsh parenting styles leave behavioral scars automatically reproducing similar dynamics without conscious examination? Maybe redirecting frustration creatively into art channels catharsis helpfully?

Either by addressing roots once perspective clears or reorienting responses, transformation unfolds. Crucially regulating speech habits prevent recurring harm. For spoken words often impact hearing psyches influentially even if uttered hastily. So a disciplined hold on tongue refining communication etiquette serves all well. Choosing consciously what words manifest upholds wisdom tradition's counsel – Right Speech avoids unverified, hurtful or idle chatter heedlessly draining vitality. Discerning speakers uplift communities.

Chapter 8 on the Law
of Humility

The second cardinal principle governing the mysterious workings of karma points towards the crucial virtue of humility regulating passage across the sea of existence.
By remaining equipoised through the shifting tides bringing alternating praise and blame, fame or disregard, gain or loss, the steady wisdom traveler traverses manifold landscapes harvesting appropriate learning without attachment. For fickle are the applauding crowds today lifted through moods suddenly shifted tomorrow.

The Law of Humility thus recommends conscious examination of life's Interdependent causal factors when enjoying success brokering deals harvesting fortunes or securing victory heroically In contested campaigns before pride arrogation goads personal credentials beyond reasonable measure. For visible attainments rest on invisible matrixes of collective merit.

The Farmer's Wisdom

When bountiful rainfall blesses crops with miracle harvests exceeding previous seasonal yields, does discerning farmer proclaim sole credit boastfully without acknowledging remote complex climate cycles granted gracious fortune? Surely elementary wisdom bending knees offers gratitude first towards

divinity marking respect for sublime workings beyond willful
control.

For overnight the same cloudbursts arbitrarily divert elsewhere
abandoning lush fields recently fertile fast transforming into
drought! Neither final victory won nor permanent defeat faced
when Interacting nature's uncertainty with equanimity. Only
perseverance continuing sensible efforts smoothly sails life's passing
phases witnessed as detached observer.

The Leader's Restraint

If through visionary conviction and charisma one inspires the
masses conversational courage transforming societies shackled by
exploitative doctrines before towards radical equality, Is pedestal
secured lifetime claiming great Messiah polyphonies sung In
posterity decisively?

Careful foresight leaves leadership arena before power's
intoxication blinds wearing humility's garment anyplace received.
For the highest truth resides not on spectacular stages furnishing
transitory ecstasies but tranquil anonymous corners sharing
beggar's transient camp fearlessly digging wisdom greater than
emperor's proud palace gained through tactful statecraft. Always
more work unfinished than trophies gathered.

The Attachment Trap

As fleeting spheres of name-form within fluctuating existence,
attachment towards accumulated possessions, achievements and
qualities spells bondage suffering inevitable separation as nothing
remains lasting.

Blinded grasping desperately even after repeatedly losing
cherished objects pains clinging, the undiscerning lament losses
lamenting woefully. While through conscious practice appreciating
impermanence, renunciation bears liberation no longer torn

between chasing after or anguished losing transient displays. Humility thus practises contentment amidst all that providence graciously bestows in each season preparing gracefully too for withdrawal when befits cycles Inexorably.

Overcoming Ego Reactions

When opinions contested breed disagreement ruffling consensus upholded before unopposed, does humility bow courteously first striving reconciliation through compassion or reactive instincts self-defensively dominate upholding image façade only?

Quick dismissing dissent arrogantly arising from fear losing imagined control authority clings, seldom yields lasting peer respect earned gently through consultative empowerment seeking cooperative truth collectively. Ego transcending response channels conflict Into constructive learning rather than destructive warfare ruinously exhausting for all Involved. Victory surely comes through letting go, never forcing.

Cultivating Gratitude

If passing privileges enjoyed like loyal friends uplifting times of need, affluent family conditions securing material comforts ahead or Innate talents magnetizing abundant opportunities owed across lifetimes ever contemplated as uncommon graces subtly supporting continuous self-development, a natural humility overwhelming heart awakens – what virtuous actions performed before ripen so fortunately now?

The awakening urges diligently Investing goodness once received back service uplifting others awaiting destiny's tide similarly turn through patient mentorship. For bounty filling possession springs countless subtle sources interdependently

weaving beyond assuming solitary cause. Treading this captured
.generosity forward multiplies blessings further

Chapter 9 on the Law of Growth

If the karmic law rings experience gained necessary fructifying lifetimes towards transcendental liberation, trying adversities require courageous embrace rather than escape when understanding opportunities spiritual progress depend integrally .upon embracing difficulties faced consciously

For unripe souls attempting quick salvatIon through pain avoidance often compounds problems blinding Insight. But sincerely accepting limitations with surrender obedience dissolves storms rendering clarity restored after temporary confusion passes. What appears random life chaos holds coded purpose revealed .gradually to waking consciousness

The Goldsmith's Wisdom

When blunt unrefined nuggets get procured Initially from dark mines scarcely resembling precious gold hidden within rough exterior, do Impatient prospectors discard back rejecting ore worthless without recognizing true metallic shine after sufficient ?fiery purification alone unlocks dormant value

Surely the discerning goldsmith commits to diligent smelting transformative process well aware through practice – crude dense matter melts giving way slowly before arising reborn gleaming precious. So too genuine seekers falter not seeing tangible progress early but surrender faithful holding vision through uncertainty periods ahead. For when hands fold away too quickly, the magician's miracle stays Interrupted abrupt even as magic waits next unfolded stroke.

The General's Insight

If naïve military commanders underestimate required wartime preparation blindly anticipating swift victory chasing glory dreams, reality delivers shocking defeats awakening truth - tangible success multiplies from strategy capital built assiduously brick by brick planned to perfection before triumphant outcomes arise visible later collectively. Raw recruits never the less committed trained rigorously through drill edging gradually finished excellence.

So too destiny unfolds incrementally seeding causes ripe collateral timed unanticipated fully through anxious minds seeking prematured control but discipline focuses steadfast on accountable task disregarding winds outcome dependent. When soul force channels unwaveringly towards envisioned goalposts victory awaits even if momentary failures meet no permanent surrender faced. For the journey alone bears fruit worthy beyond prize chased narrow..

I apologize for the confusion. You are right, when you mention to continue the next chapter, I should directly write out the full chapter content rather than just proposing an outline.

Chapter 10 on the Law of Responsibility

Whether situations faced wield control fully or demanding unwelcome adjustments breed resistant frustration, the karmic law rings declaration – one bears responsibility acting consciously uplifting destiny measured through difficulties hardly denied.

For soul cramped blaming external factors alone seeking liberation by committee committee committee shirking ownership plight extends misery awaiting deliverance birthday undelivered.While mindful self-examination redirecting that energy Inwards courageously asking what conscious response can change course considerably spreads wings once clipped by habit ignored.

By shifting lens perceiving limitation no longer barrier dividing but invitation awakening Innate potential otherwise asleep, hidden opportunities get discovered manifesting grace transcending surface futility initially presumed Intractable. For providence Indeed ordains each trial necessary strengthening self-wisdom hitherto untapped abundantly. But partial revelation waits when determination wills to look deeper beneath and beyond

The Student's Response-ability

When scholarly pursuits encounter intellectual roadblock
unable to grasp new concepts through habitual lineages of logic
tried, does seeking mind petulantly dismiss entire body of work
unreachable or respond respectfully pausing limitations before
?reorienting approach surveying matter afresh adaptive lens
Surely when mathematics hypothesis tackling
multidimensional space unyielding equations faced, Einstein shone
beacon dissolving stubborn Impasse through elevating framework
towards relativity fields explaining reality anew more
encompassingly. Every true seeker thus carries ability responding
!unconventionally to dismantle walls by building creative conduits

The Leader's Resolve

When people's elected trustee sworn constitutionally honoring
transparency governance guarding equitable society finds policy
procedures compromised seriously unable previous control, that
fiduciary responsibility refuses weak resignation but rouses
democratic resolution unflinchingly restoring order ethically no
.matter dismissals defiant faced

For when inaction fans corruption already swelling cancerous,
dharma rises up embodied Impersonally in servants of truth
scolding systemic distortion however powerful perpetrated under
facade ...by uplifting moral compass consistently due north
throughout stormy seas drenching flagship integrity temporarily
but never capsizing when crew convenes committing solidarity
.reign righteous whatever waves complicit breakers churn against

Chapter 11: The Law of Connection

The holistic lens of karma interconnects nested networks rippling across visible causality simultaneously also linking tangible efforts invested towards fruits reaped over time, beyond immediate short sightedness. By appreciating generational roots spurring opportunities taken for granted as willfully plucked privileges rather than lone survivor feats, humility arises understanding cumulative contributions manifesting personal upliftments collectively before capacities develop carriage such responsibility..

Then the driving urge rouses—what selfless service given back can empower other beings awaiting destiny's tide turn towards liberation they yearn through patient mentorship of compassion offering shoulders to stand? For inter being of shared destiny stirs conscientious response..not indifference justified through assumptions "I reclaimed myself solely so everyone determines capable similarly". Insight recognizes each context, temperament demanding unique scaffolding interventions that needful service provides without patronization..

The Farmer's Wisdom

If friendly field nymphs protect lush crops with tender care nurturing growth stealthily across seasons fulfilling plentiful harvest year upon year transferred through generations as household providence, surely through night vigil mantras invoking blessings or daybreak rituals demonstrated gratitude honoring subtle guardians that make visible prosperity feasible, invisibles too rejoice harvest shared affectionately! So consciousness bound narrow into competitive materialism obstructs livelihood, but mind liberated through spiritual respect harvesting attracts prosperity repeatedly.

The Leader's Quest

When visionary king crusading against oppressive regimes repeatedly attacking peaceful villages yearns permanently stopping the bloodbath through reconciling diplomacy, insightful ministers discerning lasting peace flows by uplifting the marginalized and addressing their insecurities urges policies preventing systemic exclusion and inequity..

For when imperial soldiers rendered unemployed desperately needing provisions for families dread conscription duty called again upon lands unlawfully wrested, uprising foments steadily from seeds suppression sown cyclically in endless wars machinery unless awakening economic empowerment or educational opportunity arise allowing ethical choice. By recognizing humanity in so called barbaric enemy and compassionately removing basis fuelling harmful ideologies, victory transcends defeating foe forcefully but uplifting all beings gradually towards justice commonweal shared.

Thus behold the cosmic dance of interdependent Karma!

Chapter 12: The Law of Focus

If destiny flows aligned towards predominant patterns we continually strengthen through motivation and exerted effort, the Karmic Law rings declaration unmistakably – energy focused prolongingly in singular direction generates considerable momentum shaping life paths ahead by force thoughts, words and actions infused.

So in stark contrast twirling merry-go-rounds spinning distraction scarcely reach anywhere, disciplined awareness harnessing intent towards noble objectives bears fruits however temporarily failures dismay during long haul perseverance demanding faith, courage and surrender before culmination arises deserved.

Yet impatient minds flit wavering through obsessions randomly bred leaping short-term pleasures merely accumulating folly amassed. Whereas concentrated consciousness penetrating truth by repeatedly reflecting underlying reality through microscope meditation or telescope wisdom maps manifesting higher vision from elevated perch.

The Sportsman's Efficiency

When determined athlete committing scheduled rigour towards focused training concentrated on strengthening weaker competencies transforms mess showing barely initial potential into medal shining demonstration peak performance garnering championships, does that sound accident or strategy meeting sweat miracles manifest? For ferocious hunger fueling consistency often turns losing odds to mouth stopped naysayers proven folly their rush judging destiny's middling journeyman yet master awakening within through unwavering self belief..

The Scientist's Breakthrough

Like steadfast researcher relentlessly testing original hypothesis against challenging orthodox paradigms facing decades of dismissive ridicule until colossal validation upturns textbook wisdom into historic discovery heralding radical shift understanding issues afresh, such alchemy transmutation too ordains faithful consciousness persevering regardless.

For verity emerges from falsehood decaying as day swallows darkest night inevitably.. Those decisive hours before dawn often seem overlong when resilience tested direfully by doubt, desperation and drudgery ahead but sincere seeking protected truth's guardian angel shepherds towards destiny once derailed remarkably. So focus anchors wandering mind ships securing safe passage however storms midway tossing.

Chapter 13: The Law of Giving and Hospitality

When virtuous consciousness awards unexpecting discriminately beneficence outpouring without restraint upholding dignity all beings equally deserving regards, providence too furnishing life purpose awakens responding kindred through synchronicities weaving deeper meaning otherwise fled awareness caught superficial accumulating trophies for glory aggrandizement alone.

So the sincere spiritualist walking talk uplifts every fallen leaf, stray animal or drainage unclogging volunteering precious lifetime's opportunities expecting least return but most needed blesses upheld occasionally by stranger's smile warming heart or wisdom glimpsed unexpectedly benefitting seeker at crossroads decisively. Thus law of karma multifold returns unasked selflessness. Detached generosity bears fruits unforeseen far greater than selfish hoard aiming extract much surrendering little unwillingly.

The Farmer's First Fruits

When celebrating harvest arrival through community event with liberal sharing abundant seasonal yield to all people without expecting immediate quid pro quo barter but invoking prosperity continuous, traditional wisdom enshrines law hospitality, gift culture and inclusive abundance flowing.

For even impoverished folk dignity stays restored through banquet brotherhood, kindred spirits nourish and visible demonstration seed yields sustained hundred folds through nature's munificence when channels jammed stinginess unclogging into largesse effused. Kindness social uplifts lives beyond siloed individualism chasing false securities miserliness breeds fearfully. Dakshina offered selflessly ritual symbols quantum harvest ahead.

The Leader's Leap of Faith

When those commanding awe inspiring authority by dint levels focus wielded productively providing visible demonstration care, faith magnifies — like Mahatma Gandhi consciously adopting simple living plus elevating 'Harijans' through skill training for self-reliance grounded nobility equality principles or King Henry IV walking barefoot penitent performing humility vows easing historical church-state frictions. Such renunciation glamour positions assumed erstwhile dissolves barriers build solidarity usher courage one-step further..

Chapter 14: The Law of Here and Now

If cosmic consciousness conjures reality through movie screens of memory past or make believe future failing fully capture unrepeatable moments flowing this very instant, urgent wisdom rings surrendering obsession recollecting glories foregoing or fantasy chasing tomorrows promised hoping golden while unraveling present stays ignored lacking luster enough......

For off-screen existence pulses powerful happiness packaged breath awaiting unboxed when awakening catalyzes suddenly through ordinary miracles abounding like toddler's infectious giggling despite thousand worries lined adult universe or mellifluous melody transcending momentarily beyond space-time bindings. Does peak experience peak seeking when parallel universes abundance glint each grain sand?

The Musician's Receptive Ear

When master performers spontaneously improvise concerts transformed through harmonizing audience energy inthralled into sanctified collective consciousness, does desperate seeking externally imposed structure regulating imagined "perfect notes" or scripted tunes diminish that creative magic? Surely mesmerized rasas manifest unpremeditated when receptive channels tuned insightfully to weave situational synergy. For the rapturous now holds eternity gleaming...

The Seeker's Presence

Like renowned philosopher J Krishnamurti repeatedly emphasize –"Truth is Pathless land" – no prepackaged techniques transmittable conceptually but only urgent attentive realization constantly diving conscious presence towards riding wave oneness, spiritual awakening too dawns alone through existential living.. Neither per formative preaching virtues from pulpits nor parroting scriptural commandments into behaviors breeds insight truly setting one free from suffering ties but repeatedly investigative questioning conditioned assumptions and social anxieties perpetuated generationally to unlock reality staring beyond..

So radical sages through time dispel maya's mirage renouncing righteous facades that virtuous pretense projects through simple childlike laughter or tears stripped naked baring essential being.. In spontaneity of pure experiencing, timeless essence arrives where seeker sought eternity escaping mortality. The law of here now upholds -This very moment ever ripe ready to reap once distraction loses allure..

Chapter 15: The Law of Change

If only certainty confronting mortality remains life's intrinsic impermanence as transient forms arise, evolve and dissolve through nature's functioning eternal cycles not pausing seasonality flux ensuring cosmic renewal continuation, wisdom flowers accepting reality as becomes rather than fantasy imagined quixotically concrete..

So spurning change by combative resistance or emotional attachment leads only undue misery clashing time's more powerful currents while adaptable resilience aligning judiciously bears peaceable fruits. Much ignorance breeds anxiety unwilling flow along as essence cannot hold permanence when manifest vehicles ever rotating transformation..

The Captain's Flexibility

When seasoned navigator steering long voyage ship discovers midway unfavorable emerging weather conditions drastically diverting preplanned course ahead recommended earlier through maritime maps, does determined leader obstinately proceed insisting or wisely adapt strategy reorienting on updated inputs that context demands saving lives and sanity all before catastrophes strike wrecking upon rocks denying obvious..

Surely emergency course corrections although humbling ego visions definitively upholding safety wisdom foremost safeguarding greater capacity regather towards destinations destiny still allows, but circuits longer may haps when fickle typhoon's winds unpaid heed blow unbereft..

The Gardener's Adaptability

When sudden monsoon floods destroy lush crops nurtured carefully through months of toil or cruel summer heat bakes inducing wilting desperation, does heart break abandoning fertile land ungratefully or renew commitment resiliently trying adaptive alternatives better suited to handle unpredictability harvested again If biodiversity ethic respects soil health through rotation methods and resilient indigenous seed varietals, possibilities sustain better than chemical shortcuts degrading.

So existence offers secure grounding but demands flexibility upheld through every trial and tribulation necessarily perfecting maturity meet phases unpredicted with equal poise.. Fault rest never adopting condition unable fully in control but entertaining fear or desperation as companion constant uninvited exhausting vitality Channels opening towards opportunity...

Chapter 16: The Law of Patience and Reward

If time's passage holds key ripening karmic fruits seeded through loving intentional actions towards benevolent ends, anxious minds enslaved chasing instant gratification lose sight slow gestating grandeur great works manifesting...Unable embrace uncertainty moments awaiting glories glimpse afore prepared..

So sages celebrating law patience extol perseverant consciousness disregarding ephemeral failure appearances patiently awaiting true victor's glory gradually emergent Sweat no small loss or meagre progress made when eyes envision splendid possibilities concealed august ahead.

But impulse seek outward security from reward less efforts undertaken undermines moral courage alone reveals treasures within. For providence times perfectly unheeded external demands push or pull through faith upheld during dark hours too.. Trust known unknown transfigures trauma into triumph assuredly..

THE FARMER'S HARVEST

When sincere tiller lab ours land lovingly through seasons without visible signs promising future harvest suddenly seeming doubt all work wasted upon stone hearted soil now unyielding more, does despair abandon fields hastily or hope keeps burning.... Faith knows through night's darkest aura often arrives brightest dawn If destiny's hands fold early before magical moment manifests then all creation's splendour stays interrupted abrupt even as miraculous fruition awaited just beyond perceiving..

So patience learns witnessing wisdom.. Storm clouds passing reflect inner state than external Andre's unmoving.. What tapasya tests today resilience strengthened galvanizes unperturbed confidence facing exponents greater aligned.... Walk on....

The Captain's Adventurous Quest..

When venturing ambitious trader risking enterprise fortune in perilous expedition unsure returns meet months yearning family left longing back home where cosy comforts familiar await, does journey await worth or anxiety defeat onboard seeking outward shores..? But discoverer's visions stoke perseverance tiding dangerous waters towards destinies still awaiting dawns early courage catalyse..

Numerous cross currents midway pose monster waves challenging still fragile barque. But captain's resilience commands crews trusting the tides ahead carry more profound yearnings than gold alone.. For when pearls purpose strung through lifetimes awaiting shine brighter emerging worth pains.. Momentary ashes often propel arising fiery wings when patience teaches learnings unforeseen.. Tough the darkest night but joy arrives dawn heralds.. Reward awaits; walk on undaunted.

Chapter 17: The Law of Significance and Inspiration

When destiny's convulsed currents cast adrift rudderless rafts title wave turmoil testing sanity's anchors amidst meaninglessness and chaos, sudden epiphanies dawn as beacon lights – either messages subconsciously arising through symbol dreams reorienting jarring journeys ahead with renewed vision or serendipities weaving coherence unexpectedly through chance encounters, aha insights or mystical graces alighting passion reigniting purpose once obscured fully..

So law unveils – no mortal limits reached without subtle significance pointer aligning higher forces conspiring upliftment cause through grace sometimes emerging least expected by grieving spirit surrendered.. For providence upholds divine meaning casting masterpiece not discard halfway should temporary inspirations wane influx routinely..

The Musician's Muse

When maestro genius composing symphonies channeling transcendence struggles through bleak arid years the divine muse untraceable by intellect's formulas alone, all striving ends waits receptive reawakening inner sight clear.. until unexpected epiphany rends veils heard only inward ear attuned.. For are masterpieces birthed wombs linear logic fully or mystic insight midwifing beauty unimagined into earthly forms..?

So Karma ripens aligned time's manifold complexity multidimensional..All living seekers traversing wisdom path accompanied invisible guides providing mentoring synchronicities unexpectedly until last summation sums all glimpsing tapestry whole however tangled separate threads appear..Trust knows brighter mornings come however dark midnight lengthens..

The Captain's North Star

When seasoned navigator steering long voyage ship discovers midway constellation compass points relied hitherto overcast unable trace course ahead, and maritime maps consulting too outdated give pause.. Dangers disorientation descend unless miraculous gift received foreshadows.. does that desperate stroke luck appear suddenly as gift grace when positivity primed or divinity's darshana dawns darkest hour reminding higher forces oversee all ventures threatening falter by strength surrendered...?

Surely uncertainty gates often require leaps faith that hesitant reason resists before triumph reveals reasons underpinning chaos.. For when mortal limits reached without subtle significance pointers realigning forces towards victory ordained, incarnate journeys too destined harbours safe however habit mind distracted interprets.. Serendipities too carve coherence unexpected through talismanic mementoes.. Luck meets those untiring upholding hopes however ensnared setbacks.. Walk on.. Persist dharma path; Divine signs ever shed light afoot when faltering loses way..

Chapter 18: The Law of Conservation

While myriad forms arise ever-changing across manifested creation's continuous dance pulsing temporal through endless cycles ceaseless, Invisible essence ever abides permanent upholding existence perennial through flux apparent. So amidst mortal frames finite strutting stages paradoxically immortal spirit
.sings unborn unceasing

Through law conservation, science extols - energy changes form but perpetuates transforming. Equally dharmic wisdom proclaims manifestation emanating the changeless essence ever same plenum ground constituting all conditionality. So individuality donned sheaths matter, lifespan and remarkable talents on loan excepting
..sole spirit force animating vehicles biological mechanical

When understanding dawns nothing absolutely eliminated but only transitioned across planes still interacting multidimensional, grief faced losing possessions or beloveds departing passing transforms embracing larger continuity Ineffable however abruptly.. What dies but for Immortal resume again..? All rivers destined meet common home ocean whichever tributary
..meandered

So psyche seeking secure permanence amidst mortal flux but reassured through law conservation upholding essence ever pristine

behind temporary turbulent changeful.. Fear loses sting
surrendering ephemeral identities once clutch desperately Into
faith timeless continuity promise ahead.. Walk on trooper.. march
..onwards warrior light

The Musician's Timeless Score

While ingenious composer scripting musical opus magnum
sees mad symphony unfinished abrupt through failing health,
insights crystallized beyond manifest creation inspires next
visionaries embellish towards perfection dreamed.. For are
Inspirations mortal framed when muse ethereal transmits
channeled unbounded? Do masterpieces emerge genius alone or
destinies awaiting manifestation select some conduits favored over
?..others its broadcast visibility Increase multi-dimensionally
Surely creation's riches conveyed particular unique expressions
losing vehicles hours does diminish what shining conduits
amplified during brief tenure or dull what still awaits revelation..
What departs conditioned existence but returns ultimately unborn
essence ever deathless.. so grieve not but celebrate undying spirit
continuously expressed ever new for aim mortal o reach immortal..
..Word made flesh uplifts towards infinity unbound

The Captain's North Star

When navigators voyaging treacherous high seas at mercy
elements lose temporarily sight orienteering constellations relied
thus far, higher cosmic order reassures through faith teaching-
traverse on unperturbed surrendering outcomes detached... For
when dilemmas darken tangled and stars shine elusive, Plough's call
...ever awaits night's clearing eventually

So law conservation reassures - God's away on business masks
larger plan whose reasons still obscure. But petty fog briefly
descends unable veil permanently essence ever perfect.. Mortal veils

cannot eclipse Immortal truths continuously broadcast awaiting reception bandwidths evolve embrace subtler signals.. Seasons flux but absolute reality shines regardless.. Have hope and keep walking.. Justice awaits.. over yonder plateau promised beholds.. Destiny fulfils even when indolence delays or storms midway toss ships apparently adrift.. Providence knows ripe time and arranges perfectly ~every fragmented Kaleidoscope piece Into magnificent mandala whole mosaic.. from perspective planes higher than
..launches Limited lens beholds through Keyholes narrow So understanding essence ever preserved beyond forms ephemeral uplifts spirit above loss sorrow deludes blinded clinging transient frames used fulfilling temporary purpose as costumes souls don.. play acting parts across existence broad.. before everyone summoned home finally boats ashore.. All call Home hear however caught market worldly echo chambers amplify possessing this transient materiality alone seals happiness secured
.eternal
Yet wisdom sound transmits– true joy abides soul freedom knowing mortal shackles Imposed merely for cosmic play.
..Deathless dignity finds devoted duty self-realization path

Chapter 19:
Understanding Today's World Using Karma

Covering cardinal laws which explain how karma as cause-effect works reorients thinking more responsibly. Now applying this wisdom on major concerns facing globally .interconnected societies allows fresh understanding

Climate Emergency Through Karma Lens

Climate crisis threatens world communities disproportionately. Poor farmers facing worst droughts or coastal villages sinking owe little fossil emissions historically. Yet relentless land exploitation valuing profits over ecological balance perpetuated blindness until alarm bells rang sinking Islands. Karma .manifests when actions disregard long term well-being

Seeing humanity interlinked sharing planetary home rather than self-centered control, humility arises. Steps upholding justice aim lifestyle changes beyond carbon neutrality. Shifting trillions in subsidies funding petro-economy urgently towards green energy access empowers excluded majority resilience staying worst climate turmoil ahead. Their voices lead reconciliation heal divided world. .Karma fruits transform when ethics guides economics

Healing Historical Wrongs Using Karma

Oppression leaving unhealed wounds breeds collective trauma across generations even after official redress. Without adequately addressing deep Inequities built from slavery, colonial abuses, native displacements, reconciliation rings hollow allowing Inequality and prejudice perpetuate subtly. Karma cannot ignore ill-gotten gains continuing benefit some disproportionately on backs broken crying for justice.

True healing needs truth-facing, redistributive repair and structural reform. Not celebrating exploiters of yesterday as heroes just because history judges complex. By memorializing tragedy which triumph cost, dignity restores when descendants lead mourning rituals, reclaim erased Identity on restituted land rights towards resilient future sowing peace. Karma transforms upholding moral courage

Reimagining Technology and Karma

Digital revolution holds wonderful connectivity yet worsens inequality and confusion. Social media steers outrage Algorithmic echo chambers block real understanding across lines. Speed pressure valorizes reactive anger outpacing wisdom. Who controls .data, codes, networks controls power often heedless of harm Wisdom tradition teaches technology itself has no inherent bias except what creators consciously build. Upholding timeless values like truth-seeking beyond propaganda, empathy building Inclusive identities beyond divisive othering, cooperation not extractive profit in designing systems spreads universal benefit. Karma outcomes elevate when ethics Informs engineering for ..common dignity

Chapter 20: Beacons of Light – Positive Influencers Manifesting Karma

While cardinal laws unravel karma's subtle workings, inspiring figures across history embody uplifting change through walking courageous talk serving most vulnerable oppressed against staggering odds. By examining exemplary lives, understand better our shared potential consciously altering unjust systems breeding Indignity, oppression or violence passed down through collective ignorance, indifference and prejudice across generations. Reformation awaits unleashing radical wisdom and love.

Jane Addams (1860-1935) Winds of Change

Ever since 1881 visiting foul English slums, prosperous young Jane envisioned pioneering poverty alleviation back home by co-founding Hull House In troubled Chicago neighborhood as settlement uplifting immigrants using arts, activism and ecology improvement. Gradually seed grew mighty oak. Addams' sincere kindness mingling, listening, learning and lifting touched thousands in need through community kitchens, anti-child labor fights and women's suffrage marches. Her inclusive cooperative spirit weaving solidarity inspired social work profession emerging. Even securing 1931 Nobel peace prize for pacifist writing worldwide. Where need appears, love responds - Addams kept sowing change.

Jiddu Krishnamurti (1895-1986) – Truth is Pathless Land World teacher fame awaited 14 year old Krishnamurti as Messiah head Theosophy before his radical Insight dissolved Order shocking followers preferring fearless truth-seeking over packaged salvation solutions mindlessly perpetuated. Thereafter for six prolific decades globally, Krishnamurti penetrated conditioned egoistic mindsets which breed violence, nationalism exposing individual responsibility revolutionize consciousness elevating society holistically beyond reform fragmented institutions unable address root prejudices cultural religious perpetuated Ignorance, hatred. Through public talks Insistently deconstructing psychological mechanisms erecting divisions, creating images binding identities defensively he awakened many towards seeing collective suffering Inseparably, citing change must emerge understand oneself meditatively.

Wangari Maathai (1940 – 2011) Greening Conscience After being first central African woman earning doctorate toggling challenges of single parenthood and battling cancer, academic Wangari pIoneered sustainable Greenbelt Pan African reforestation movement uplifting women environmental stewards. Planting over 50 million trees with grassroots collectives Kenya addressing fuel-wood needs and community livelihood creatively aligned ancient eco-feminine wisdom values manifesting food sovereignty resisting corporate land grab. For such seeding conscience work upholding earth democracy symbiotically Maathai endured beatings, jail yet persevered smiling through

Nobel peace prize 2004 heralding holistic environmentalism Integrating restorative justice with land ethics benefitting most dispossessed.

Medha Patkar (1954 -) Flowing with People's Power

Leaving academic career midway risked then unknown Medha dedicate her strategic pioneering brilliance completely working with Indigenous tribal protesting mammoth Sardar Sarovar Narmada dam construction submerging fertile ancestral farms towards uncertain rehabilitation, by researching relentlessly building evidence human rights violations from callous development project funded questionable means. Her nonviolent Gandhian appeals persistently pressuring courts stalling decades alongside advocating energy democracy decentralizing electricity access uplifting climate justice beyond urban Industrial lobby demands manifesting partially through sympathetic recent judicial rulings easing displaced rehabilitation after prolonged struggle now inspirational model advocating precedent. Patience with deep grassroots solidarity bears fruits ripened in time.

Uplifting Change-Makers Manifesting Karma

Beyond theorizing karmic principles abstractly lies witnessing moral causality unfold through courageous figures who confronted unethical status quos directly. By revisiting few such agents of hope who catalyzed social justice reforms democratizing dignity for many awaiting Integrated destiny's tide serving oppressed, fresh perspectives emerge on Individual responsibility towards collective upliftment we all share as planetary citizens bound seeking liberation Inseparable.

Jane Addams: Weaving Women's Wisdom

Unlike rushed messiahs proclaiming revolutions overnight, change seeded enduringly arises from cooperative efforts building common ground listening, educating and activating community from grassroots gradually. The historic lasting Impact trailblazer Jane Addams made uplifting disempowered immigrant groups through Hull settlement house anchors lasting wisdom. Her creative citizenship schools fostering cultural pride, multilingual lectures for capability building, theatre nourishing empathy beyond xenophobia, trade union advocacy securing workers rights and even risking arrest marching against World War's destructive hubris set powerful precedents on social work's potential reconciling communities towards progressive sustainable living. .Patient cumulative efforts weave destinies positively

Chapter 21: Evolving Karma – Wisdom Tools for Better Living

Beyond fatalistic notions that karma binds beings helplessly with predetermined fate, the empowering insight across Dharmic traditions recognizes everyone retains power reshaping destiny regardless present scenarios faced through exercising intentional choices uplifting thoughts, words and actions from ignorant unconscious patterns causing suffering to conscious vows alleviating world's profound inequities.

For denominators undergirding collective misery – poverty, exploitation, conflict, fear – breed perpetuating cycles dehumanization until bold beings question courageously unjust status quos asking – "How might injustices plaguing humanity end if each person awakened seeing our shared dignity inalienably?" This mindset shift flows from profound metaphysic – each existence unfolding here ripens unimaginable causality spanning vast interconnections across space time beyond just isolated individuality so however downtrodden by Parker's unjust,1234 redemption ever awaits willing agency committed steadfast reforming systems meaningfully start where stands through wisdom and compassion..

By understanding key levers influencing karmic creation and dissolution, one gains liberating means reforming habitual tendencies currently binding problems. Light awaits gleaming beyond tunnel darkness when sincere sight seeks..

Mental Models: Shaping Thought Habits

Cognitive patterns continually focused anxiety, lack or resentment maintain miseries chained rather than cultivating gratitude, abundance and goodwill gradually transforming indolent egos towards generosity compassion uplifting all beings equally. So conscientiously reconditioning assumptions about people, possibilities and life's deeper meaning allows fresh perspectives dissolving long perpetuated ignorance blindly.

Examining conditioned prejudices, rushing reactive anger habitually without allowing empathetic pause first damages relations though seeming justified short sighted. But uplifting vision recognizes shared struggles search dignity blade complex causes perpetuating suffering until consciousness rests seeing humanity's shared grace ultimately. Patience focused reforming systems oppression then bears fruits ripening differently than quick fix revolution attempts alone sparing little change deeply.

SPEECH MINDFULLY SEASONED

When impatience breeds reactionary outbursts defensively before we investigate trigger issues calmer or petulant blame projecting failure unpleasantly arise, contemplative efforts pausing deeply why particular situations recurrently evoke such patterns reveal much. Perhaps harsh parenting styles leave behavioral scars automatically reproducing similar dynamics without conscious examination? Maybe redirecting frustration creatively into art channels catharsis helpfully?

Either by addressing roots once perspective clears or reorienting responses, transformation unfolds. Crucially regulating speech habits prevent recurring harm. For spoken words often impact hearing psyches influentially even if uttered hastily. So a disciplined hold reigning tongue while refining communication etiquette serves all well. Choosing consciously what words manifest uplifts wisdom tradition's counsel – Right Speech avoids unverified, hurtful or idle chatter needlessly draining vitality. Discerning speakers spread communal harmony.

Action Helping Hands

While mental models unconsciously perpetuate ignorance verbal expressions manifest unprocessed hurt outwardly, actions directly impact realities faced through results self and others receive. Beyond lamenting harsh news bred apathy, wisdom recognizes — unjust systems imprinted over generations also supply leverage points where conscious choice alters course gradually. Karma fruits transform through perseverant effort however hidden such alternate levers appear initially until deeper discernment guides view afresh..

So three forms uplifting action empty misery's immense oceans — ceasing actions directly recreating harmful patterns heedlessly, initiating skillful responses dissolving ignorance with empathy and wisdom seeding interdependence and persevering urgency highest conscience commands despite steep odds change ripens.. only through radical collaboration upholding solidarity realizing shared justice inseparably.

Micro worlds: Reshaping Home Habits

When young minds absorb unconscious fears or harmful assumptions through traditions unquestioned critically, cycles prejudice fester leakage families alone unable contain without reconciling adult accountability ills perpetuated under guise conforming disciplines harsh. So conscious wisdom blooms examining tender roots by acknowledging intergenerational trauma haunting elder psyche manifesting reactive abuse. For when psychological nutrition denied core, why expect comfort fruits nourished public persona fronts while insecurity festers backstage..

So truth reconciliation restoring communication channels breeds healing gradually fear barriers clouding giving way when naming shadow integrates admitting harms inflicted and humility seeks making thoughtful amends.. Wise progenitors uplift little spirits fortifying footfalls towards destiny abundant through nurturing self esteem not enforcing irrational demands perfecting fail.. This lifts both old and young through patience. Loving guidance over domination allows innate talents manifestation channeling unique genius trajectories unimagined..

Macro worlds: Overhauling Systems

If global Living victories call for application ethical principles broadly practices what inner wisdom gleans, embodied realization demands uplifting outward forms too existing mirrored collective beliefs perpetuated.. systems laws lifestyles artwork habits traditions unmindfully absorbed need cleansing alignment wisdom discovered within.. since worlds interbeing revelations providence unveils in solitude gains fuller external fruition when embedded cultural matrices integrate similarly altering..

So activists guide revolutions overturning unjust structures oppressively enforced give way for restorative alternatives where each being participates freedom dignity intact because shared divinity glimmers all manifestations same transcendental source.. Governance reshaped ensures inclusive participation historically marginalized upholding talents overlooked by maintaining mediocre status quos.. policies encourage conservation of common assets air water knowledge equitably accessible through decentralizing frameworks shaped.. technologies respecting sentience biological cultural boundaries channel progress ways upholding sustainability enrichment all forms existence our kin.. commerce flows circular economy nourishing prosperity equitably cooperative uplifting communities creatively not capital means alone dictating lopsided shareholder wealth.. redesigned urban spaces integrate greening models make earth democracy real starting neighborhoods bottom-up..

When young visionaries renounce careerism opting grassroots apprenticeship purpose learning participatory frameworks, collective merit accrues for timely solutions ripen.. so intellectual elites too often fortifying ivory privilege find urgent meaning realigning resources reforming unjust constructs wasting planet's precious progress opportunities accelerate..

Ripening Time Now

For modern complex interconnectivity global now interlinks humanity's actions inextricably across once distanced geographies. Pandemics prove CLEAN how uprooted trees miles away threaten biodiversity balances delicately enabling zoonosis springs wipe prosperity decades built through mindless deforestation..Media streams visually document climate refugees immisserated when industrial addiction drains African lakes dry.. So aggregate karma ripens unknowably vast operating through myriad seen unseen causes..

No soul can predict definitely life's karmic fruits ahead by tallying specific efforts and external fortunes arbitrarily. But by channeling consciousness continuously upholding virtue ethics, wisdom teachers reassure existence reveals purpose and justice... If not immediately then over beyond horizons vision limited..Walk On undaunted patience!

Chapter 22: Wisdom's Call – Transforming Destiny by Living Karma Consciously

Imagine strolling ancient Indian Himalayan foothills when suddenly cloudburst drenches your little village sweeping precious topsoil downhill altering life patterns earned through generations farming orchards..What fate awaited peripatetic grandma now climate refugee marching unsure futures now that angry rivers swallowed up ancestral home nurturing continuity tradition temple tales existed! Do karmic debts accrued inadvertently jeopardize her clan towards impoverishment when elder survival itself at stake hood homeless? Yet haven awaits in compassionate Sikh shelter voluntarily built uphill by conscious diaspora youth heeding solidarity service call.. For providence conspires uplifting ways unpredicted beforehand through our inextricably shared being on sentient Earth..

So unravels ongoing human spectacle.. Unborn threads invisible causes woven consequences rippling families across seas outside observable ganders exclaiming shock-"how one reaps unknowable beyond narrow gaze backwards our solitary effort" since destiny interweaves too subtly realize fully.. Yet free will dangles enticingly upholding choice – repeat unconscious patterns leashed habits generations perpetuate or stall vicious cycles pausing consciously..

Turbulent unfolding's confront all mortals ultimately – loss unanticipated, up heavements suddenly dismantling stable terrains financial or families anchoring securities emotional..No soul escapes tasting bitter life potions time's alchemy serves each seeking homecoming last..

But perspectives shape response – either constrict awareness hurriedly rebuilding while lamenting temporary sustenance embittered before billows next swash away sandcastles.. Or illumine courageously upholding possibilities inspired anew seeing fresh track arising while accepting limitation nonattached.. Renouncing resistance calm emerges; Patience ripens insight..

For divine play unfolds every scene meticulously before curtain falls complete last act..So fret not but witness flow trustingly one chosen surrendered instrument vast orchestral symphony.. Trifles daily offer turn awakening..Walk on trooper undaunted.. Justice awaits over yonder plateau promised beholds..

So what strange phenomenon binds humanity its comedy across millennia generations yearning freedom yet forging fates fettered through ignorance delusion perpetuated cyclically lifetimes until Sahasrara liberation dawns seventh peak transcending wheels Samsara entirely? Why universal themes fears anxieties cling despite habitats histories cultures or privilege economic now digitally interlinked global family?? What unconscious forces continue breeding destruction often despite best intentioned idealistic interventions superficially applied ushering paradise but paving pathways actually hell?!

Behind visible formations geology plate tectonics, biological species botanical celestial, through unseen dimensions infinite expansion levels atoms galaxies..wise seers point unified theory.. A profound fractal resonance undergirds manifested phenomena.."Yat Pinde tat Brahmande"..Energies vitalizing body cosmos identically operate through principle cause-effect sowing fruits seeds patterned intricately.. ancients termed 'Karma' interpretive key making coherent sense joy and suffering's unequal distribution all beings traversing realms time and space walk paths unique yet unified source all emerges.. Creativity destructivity twin dance Shiva..Unveil masks perceive singular essence dawning myriad names-forms..Tat Tvam Asi..That Self You Become..Knock doors hidden exploited selves heal schisms without..

So Karma offers holistic framework integrating diversity conscious expression evolving through cycles vast comprehend fully yet pivotal wisdom liberates.. By understanding habits perpetuating harmful ignorae generating collective misery or cocreating alternatives that uplift dispossessed healing historic divides, one grasps innate power reshape destiny and dharma – ethical action liberating suffering sentience..

Does cynicism breed feeling helpless crisis compounding daily or optimism potency within to redirect course human progression away self extinction the tipping point calibration awaits pioneers awaken Wisdom reconciling head heart courageously innovating governance frameworks integrate complexity challenges now evolves species Saturn's next rings or mars sooner than sustainable paradise envisioned.. exporting excesses progress few prospered at expense depredating our shared ecology support web interbeing now dawning minds awakened recognize reality one spirit donning costumes culture while forgetting temporarily source essence we share equally divine ultimately..

Walk in beauty; Choices follow..

THE END

Don't miss out!

Visit the website below and you can sign up to receive emails whenever Loryan wenny publishes a new book. There's no charge and no obligation.

https://books2read.com/r/B-A-CEWDB-FDZWC

BOOKS 2 READ

Connecting independent readers to independent writers.